W9-BWC-126

Greenacres Library

SEP 2 6 2006

J 746 .434 RON
Ronci, Kelli.
Kids crochet : projects
for kids of all ages /

PALM BEACH COUNTY
LIBRARY SYSTEM
3650 SUMMIT BLVD.
WEST PALM BEACH, FLORIDA 33406

Kids Crochet

Kelli Ronci

Photographs by John Gruen

Illustrations by Lena Corwin

STC CRAFT | A MELANIE FALICK BOOK   NEW YORK

For mom and dad—my first teachers.

Text copyright © 2005 Kelli Ronci
Illustrations copyright © 2005 Lena Corwin
Photographs copyright © 2005 John Gruen

All rights reserved. No portion of this book may be reproduced, stored in a retrieval system, or transmitted in any form or by any means, mechanical, electronic, photocopying, recording, or otherwise, without written permission from the publisher.

Published in 2005 by
STC Craft | A Melanie Falick Book
115 West 18th Street
New York, NY 10011
www.abramsbooks.com

Canadian Distribution:
Canadian Manda Group
One Atlantic Avenue, Suite 105
Toronto, Ontario M6K 3E7
Canada

Library of Congress Cataloging-in-Publication Data
Ronci, Kelli.
  Kids crochet : projects for kids of all ages / Kelli Ronci ;
photographs by John Gruen ; illustrations by Lena Corwin.
    p. cm.
  Includes index.
  ISBN 1-58479-413-5
  1. Crocheting--Juvenile literature. I. Title.

TT820.R743 2005
746.43'4--dc22
2004017477

The text of this book was composed in Sauna designed by Underware

Printed in Singapore
10 9 8 7 6 5 4 3 2 1
FIRST PRINTING

Stewart, Tabori & Chang is a subsidiary of

LA MARTINIÈRE
GROUPE

Edited by Melanie Falick
Designed by Jennifer Wagner
Production by Alexis Mentor

Introduction

Have you ever imagined making a piece of fabric with your own hands?

This book will show you how. Crochet (which rhymes with *okay*), like its cousin knitting, is a way of creating fabric by pulling one loop of yarn through another. In knitting, this is done with two needles, but in crochet it's done with just a single hook.

No one knows exactly who invented crochet. What we do know is that the word "crochet" is actually the French word for *hook*, and around the 16th century, French nuns began making lace using a needle with a hook on one end. Over the years, crochet has gone in and out of style, but nowadays it's so popular that many people are forming crochet clubs — there's even a national crochet club that hosts a race to see who can crochet the fastest!

In *Kids Crochet*, you'll learn everything you need to know to make things that you can wear, like hats, scarves, and sweaters, as well as fun accessories and toys that make great gifts. Your friends and family are sure to be happy to receive handmade treasures that you've created especially for them. Most of the fourteen projects are so small and simple that you'll be able to complete them in one or two sittings, while a few will need to be done over time, or with some help from your friends.

Once you learn how to crochet, I bet you'll want to teach it to all of your friends. My friend Steffi taught me how to crochet. When Steffi was very young, she taught herself how to crochet a cactus by looking at one of her mother's books. It wasn't long before she was crocheting up a storm, making clothes for her dolls, and eventually a sweater for herself. Crochet can be a very addictive hobby! Once you get the hang of it, and your fingers get into the rhythm, it's hard to stop! Luckily, you can crochet just about anywhere—indoors or outdoors, on the bus, or in the car.

Each chapter in *Kids Crochet* introduces a new skill with colorful step-by-step illustrations that are easy to follow. You'll learn how to make stitches, switch colors, and create different textures and shapes — soon you'll be on your way to creating your very own crochet designs.

I had a great time teaching all of the children in the photos in this book how to crochet, and they taught me a lot about how to be a better teacher. For most of them, it was only a couple of hours before they were crocheting like pros! Now you too can benefit from what we all learned together. There's nothing more rewarding than making something with your own hands.
Prepare to get "hooked" on crochet!

Attention Lefties

Both hands are important when you crochet, and that's why many left-handed people are able to learn how to crochet by following the same instructions as their right-handed friends. However, if you are left-handed and the instructions in this book feel awkward to you, don't give up! First, using a pencil, cross out "right hand" in the instructions and write in "left hand." Then, prop up the book in front of a mirror, so that the illustrations are reversed, and switch to holding the hook in your left hand and the working yarn in your right hand.

getting
started!

A ball of yarn—that's all you need
to get started learning how to crochet.
You won't need a crochet hook at first, because you can
begin learning the basic principle of crochet—how to
hook one loop through another—right on your fingers.
The first step is to choose a yarn that you'll enjoy
working with. In the next few pages you'll learn how
to wind a ball of yarn (with a little help from a friend),
what animals and plants the different types
of yarns come from, how to identify the tools used
in crochet, and how to make finger crochet chains
and turn them into fun accessories.

Wind Up!

Together, Fiona and Sadie-Mae wind a ball of yarn so they can begin crocheting.

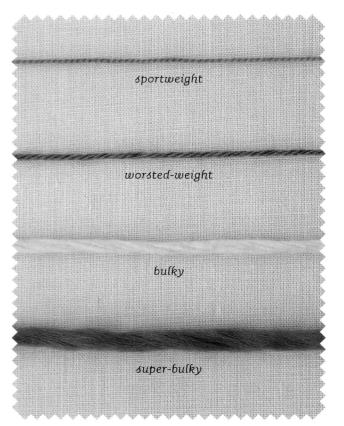

sportweight

worsted-weight

bulky

super-bulky

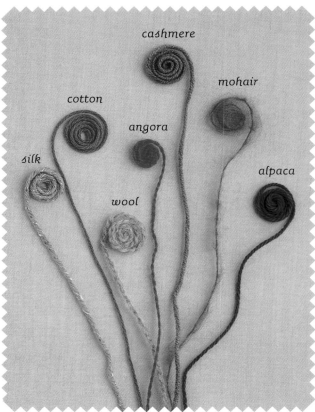

cashmere

mohair

cotton

angora

silk

alpaca

wool

Don't Forget!

If you are choosing yarn for a project that you will wear next to your skin, such as a scarf, be sure you like the way it feels. To test the yarn before buying it, hold it up to your neck or cheek or another sensitive spot on your body.

choosing yarns and tools

HERE'S SOME IMPORTANT INFORMATION ABOUT THE YARN
AND TOOLS YOU NEED TO GET STARTED LEARNING HOW TO CROCHET.
ALL OF THESE MATERIALS ARE SOLD AT YARN AND CRAFT STORES.

choosing yarn

There are two things to keep in mind when choosing a yarn to work with. First, make sure you love everything about it—the color, and the way it feels in your hands. Try to work with light-colored, smooth yarns when you are learning, so that it will be easy for you to see your stitches. Next, be sure to pick a yarn that is the correct weight for the project you are going to make. The terms "sportweight," "worsted-weight," "bulky," and "super-bulky" are general categories that refer to the thickness of the yarn, and most yarn labels list one of these terms. The yarns in the picture at left will help you identify the type of yarn to use for the projects in the following chapters.

Winding a Ball of Yarn

Some yarn comes in a skein (rhymes with "rain") twisted in a figure-8 shape. If you try to work directly from the skein, the yarn will become tangled. Before you begin, you'll need to wind it into a ball. Untwist the skein so that it forms one big loop. Then place it over the back of a chair, or a friend's outstretched arms (see photo on page 7). Cut any small pieces of yarn that might be tied around the skein, and then find one of the ends. To get the ball started, wrap the yarn around your hand about 20 times to form a small bundle, then slip it off your hand and wind the yarn around the center of the bundle another 20 times. Turn the bundle slightly and wind another 20 times. Continue to turn the bundle and wind the remainder of the skein.

Where Does Yarn Come From?

SOME YARNS ARE MADE FROM NATURAL FIBERS THAT COME FROM ANIMALS AND PLANTS. THE PHOTO ON THE RIGHT ON PAGE 8 SHOWS SEVEN TYPES OF NATURAL FIBER YARN. THE PICTURE HERE SHOWS THEIR ORIGINAL HOSTS.

Cashmere comes from the undercoat of a cashmere goat, *alpaca* from an alpaca (a relative of the camel), *mohair* from an angora goat, and *angora* from an angora rabbit. *Wool* yarn comes from different kinds of sheep, but the softest comes from merino sheep. *Silk* is cultivated from the cocoon of the silkworm, and *cotton* is harvested from the cotton plant. Nowadays, many yarns are also made either entirely from chemicals called synthetics, the most common being acrylic, or by combining synthetic and natural fibers together. Some people like to work with synthetic yarn because it can be less expensive than natural yarn, and is machine washable (most natural yarns need to be washed by hand). However, many people prefer to work with natural yarns because they look and feel so nice!

Planning a Field Trip

It's always lots of fun to see fiber-producing animals in person. To find farms near where you live, try calling your local 4-H Club, chamber of commerce, zoo, or even yarn shops in your area. Chances are someone who works in these places will be able to lead you in the right direction.

choosing tools

crochet hooks

Crochet hooks come in many sizes, and each one is marked with a letter, or a number followed by "mm" (the abbreviation for millimeters) to indicate its size. The skinnier the hook, the lower the letter (or number); the fatter the hook, the higher the letter (or number). Crochet hooks are often sold in sets, and it's a good idea to purchase them this way, so that you'll have a variety of different sizes to choose from when working on the projects in this book. The size of the hook that you work with, combined with the thickness of the yarn that you choose, will affect the overall look and feel of your crochet.

scissors

Choose scissors that can cut through yarn easily. Try not to use the same pair to cut through paper, as this will dull the blades.

yarn needle

You will need a yarn needle for sewing pieces of crochet together and to weave in the yarn tails. Also known as tapestry needles, they come in a couple of sizes, and in metal or plastic. They look like really big sewing needles with a large eye and a less pointy tip.

tape measure or ruler

A regular 12-inch ruler will work for measuring small pieces of flat crochet, but to measure larger pieces you will need a tape measure.

split-ring stitch markers (or safety pins)

A split-ring stitch marker is a small plastic ring with an opening on one side. Stitch markers help you to keep track of where you are in a pattern. They are made with an opening on one end so they can be slipped directly onto the front loop of a stitch. As an alternative, you can use a safety pin.

pins

You will use pins to pin down your finished crochet pieces to be "blocked"—a process that helps your crochet lay flat and look nice. Straight pins with round plastic tips work well for pinning pieces of crochet, because they won't slip through the stitches, and are easy to remove. T-pins, which look like the letter T, also work well.

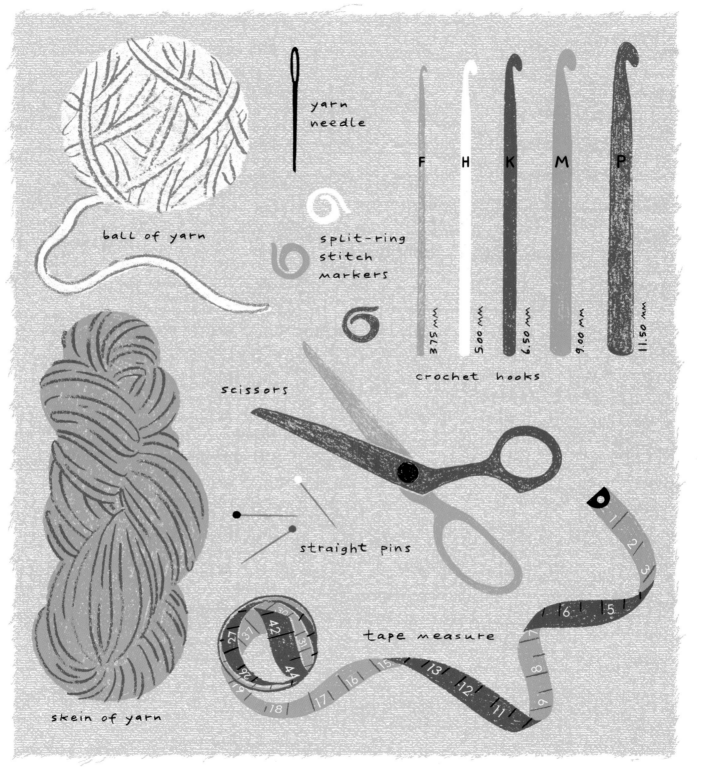

ball of yarn

yarn
needle

split-ring
stitch
markers

F H K M P

3.75 mm
5.00 mm
6.50 mm
9.00 mm
11.50 mm

crochet hooks

scissors

straight pins

tape measure

skein of yarn

finger crochet

BEFORE LEARNING TO CROCHET WITH A HOOK, TAKE SOME TIME TO PRACTICE MAKING CHAINS ON YOUR FINGERS. IT PROBABLY WON'T TAKE MORE THAN A FEW MINUTES TO MASTER THE TECHNIQUE OF CONNECTING ONE LOOP TO ANOTHER.

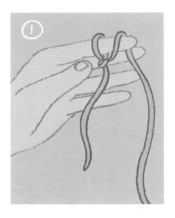 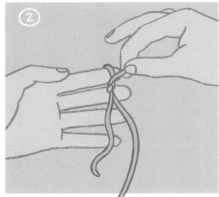 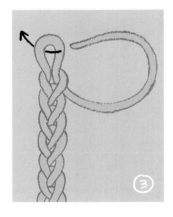

1 Tie the yarn around your index finger in a double knot, and let the tail (the short end of the yarn) fall into the palm of your hand. Wrap the working yarn (the yarn coming from the ball) over the tip of your index finger, from front to back, so that it is right next to the tied yarn on your finger.

2 With your other hand, pull the tied loop of yarn over the wrapped strand of yarn, and off your finger, so you are left with 1 loop on your finger again. Repeat steps 1 and 2 several times, and you will soon begin to see a crocheted *chain* forming.

3 When your chain is as long as you want it to be, take your finger out and cut the working yarn a few inches from the end of the chain. Thread the end of the yarn through the last loop, and pull it tight.

To hide the tails at the beginning and end of the chain, use a yarn needle to weave them back and forth through the loops on the back of the chain a few times. Then cut the ends close of the chain, being careful not to cut through your stitches.

There are a lot of fun things you can do with your chains. Try making a bunch in different colors and yarn weights. You can turn them into bracelets to trade with your friends by using the leftover tails to tie the ends together around your wrist, or try wrapping a few chains around an empty bottle or jelly jar to make a pretty vase or pencil holder. All you need is some white glue to hold the chains in place. Long chains tied in a bow around gift boxes are a fun alternative to ribbon, and skinny chain shoelaces made from cotton yarn with pony beads on the ends will dress up your shoes.

crochet
with a hook

Get ready to learn the basic steps
for crocheting with a hook: how to attach
the yarn to the hook with a slipknot; how to hold the
crochet hook; how to make a chain with a hook
(just like you did with your fingers in the last chapter);
and then how to do the single crochet stitch, the stitch
that is used to make every project in this book.
Before you know it, you'll be finishing up your first project:
a small scarf called a Neck Cozy or a Tool Pouch.
To learn these techniques, it's a good idea to work with
a big hook (size N or P) and bulky yarn.

Attach the Yarn to the Hook With a Slipknot

THE FIRST STEP IN CROCHETING WITH A HOOK IS ATTACHING YOUR YARN TO THE HOOK. YOU DO THIS WITH A SIMPLE SLIPKNOT. THERE ARE A LOT OF DIFFERENT WAYS TO MAKE A SLIPKNOT. THE TECHNIQUE SHOWN HERE IS REALLY EASY BUT IF YOU ALREADY KNOW HOW TO MAKE A SLIPKNOT A DIFFERENT WAY, GO AHEAD.

1 Wrap the yarn around the index and middle fingers of one hand, so that it's looped around your fingers and crossed in front of them like an "X." Make sure the "working yarn" (the yarn attached to the ball) is crossing over the "tail" (the short end of the yarn). The tail should be about 5 inches long.

2 With your other hand, slip your fingers under the "X" and pull the working yarn up through the yarn looped on your fingers, creating a second loop.

3 Put the tip of the hook through this second loop, from back to front, and pull your index and middle fingers out of the first loop.

4 Gently pull on both the tail and the working yarn to form the slipknot, then pull the working yarn to tighten the loop on the hook.

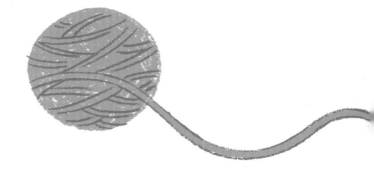

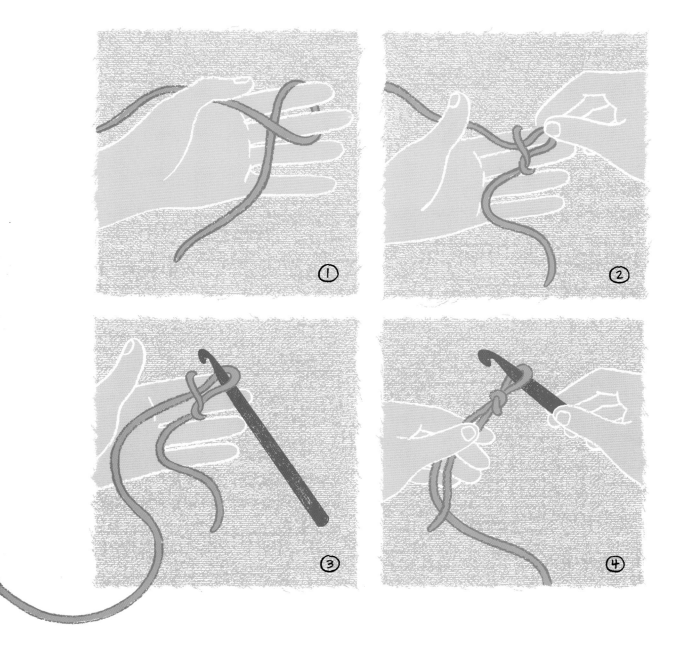

Holding the Hook and Yarn

LEARNING HOW TO HOLD YOUR HOOK AND YARN IS AN IMPORTANT PART OF LEARNING TO CROCHET. IN ORDER TO MAKE BEAUTIFUL, EVEN STITCHES, YOU WANT TO KEEP YOUR HANDS RELAXED AND IN POSITION. AT FIRST, THE POSITIONS SHOWN HERE MAY FEEL A BIT AWKWARD, BUT LEARNING HOW TO HOLD THE HOOK IS A LOT LIKE LEARNING HOW TO RIDE A BIKE, OR TIE YOUR SHOES — WITH PRACTICE, YOU'LL START TO GET THE HANG OF IT, AND IT WILL FEEL MORE NATURAL.

1 Always start by attaching the yarn to the hook with a slipknot (see page 18). Then, hold the hook in your right hand like it's an ice cream scoop. Make sure the center of the hook is in between your thumb and index finger, the end of the hook is inside your palm, and the tip of the hook is facing you.

2 With your left hand, palm facing down, hook the working yarn first with your pinky, and then hook it again with your index finger. The yarn should pass over your pinky, under your 2 middle fingers, and over your index finger. *Remember, the working yarn is the yarn attached to the ball.*

3 Then turn your palm to face you. The working yarn will stretch across the inside of your hand.

4 Hold the slipknot on the hook between the thumb and middle finger of your left hand, keeping your index finger up. Let go of your hook for a second and reach behind your left hand to pull down on the working yarn, tightening it around your index finger. *Make sure not to pull too tight. The yarn should stretch across your index finger at a comfortable distance from the hook.*

Now you are ready to begin crocheting with a hook!

Working Up Speed

It may seem hard to believe when you're first learning, but the fastest crocheter in the world can work over 90 stitches in a minute!

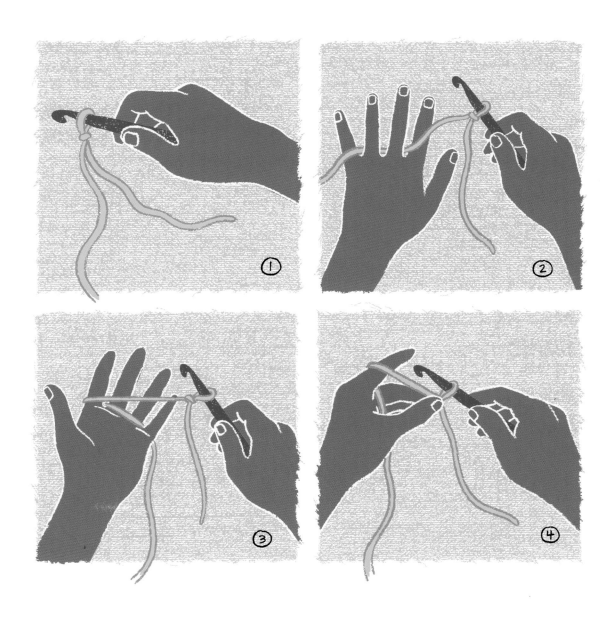

Chain Stitch

IN CROCHET, LOOPS OF YARN ARE HOOKED TOGETHER, LIKE THE LINKS IN A CHAIN.
IN FINGER CROCHET (PAGE 14), YOU MADE EACH LINK IN THE CHAIN BY WRAPPING
THE YARN AROUND YOUR FINGER AND PULLING ONE LOOP THROUGH THE NEXT.
NOW YOU WILL USE THE HOOK, INSTEAD OF YOUR FINGERS, TO DO THE SAME THING.
ALWAYS BEGIN BY ATTACHING THE YARN TO THE HOOK WITH A SLIPKNOT (PAGE 18),
AND BY GETTING INTO POSITION WITH YOUR HOOK AND YARN (PAGE 20).

1 Wrap the working yarn around the hook, from *back to front*. (Make sure you don't wrap the yarn from front to back — this will make your stitches too tight).

2 Catch the yarn inside the tip of the hook, and pull it down through the loop on the hook. *If the loop on the hook is too tight, gently pull down on the slipknot to loosen it and make room for your hook to pass through.*

You've made one chain stitch! Now move your thumb and middle finger up to hold the chain stitch you just made, and gently pull down on it to loosen the loop around the hook.

3 Repeat steps 1 and 2, until the chain is the length you want it to be. Each stitch should look like a "V." To count your stitches, start with the first "V" next to the hook, and count down to the last "V" at the tip of the chain. *The loop on the hook and the knot at the end do not count as stitches.*

Take a look at your chain. Are the stitches big and loose, or are they small and tight? Most people make their first chain stitches a little too tight, but you want to make sure your stitches are big enough to put the hook back through them. If your stitches are too tight, you may be holding the working yarn too tight, or wrapping it around the hook in the wrong direction. The trick is to keep your hands relaxed, and let the working yarn pass freely through your left hand, always making sure it is stretched across your index finger at a comfortable distance from the hook. Keep practicing until you are able to make even chain stitches that are big and loose, and remember to always wrap the yarn from *back to front* on the first step.

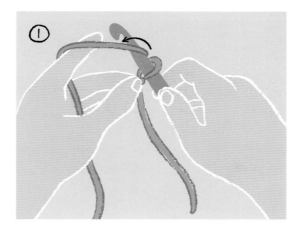

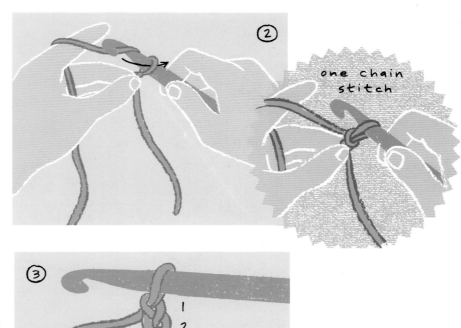

one chain
stitch

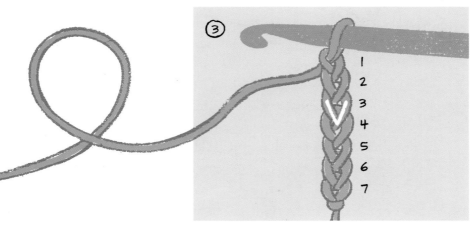

1
2
3
4
5
6
7

Single Crochet

IN CROCHET, THERE ARE MANY DIFFERENT KINDS OF STITCHES,
BUT THE MOST BASIC IS CALLED "SINGLE CROCHET." TO GET THE HANG OF
SINGLE CROCHET, MAKE A TEST SAMPLE (CALLED A SWATCH).

1 Attach the yarn to the hook with a slip-knot (page 18), and get into position with your hook and yarn (page 20). Make a row of 11 chain stitches (see instructions on page 22). This is called the "foundation row."

To begin single crochet, skip over the first chain stitch next to the hook and put the hook through the second chain stitch, from front to back.

2 Wrap the yarn around the hook from *back to front*, and pull it through the first loop on the hook so that you have 2 loops on the hook.

3 Wrap the yarn around the hook from *back to front* again, and pull it through both of the loops on the hook.

4 You've made one single crochet stitch! Now repeat steps 1 through 3, making one single crochet stitch in each chain stitch of your foundation row.

5 At the end of the row, take a close look at the top of your stitches. Notice how the top of each single crochet stitch is V-shaped.

Count each "V" to make sure you have the right number of stitches. If you began with a chain of 11 stitches, you should now have 10 single crochet stitches.

6 To begin the next row, turn your work over from right to left, the same way you would turn the pages of a book, and make one chain stitch.

7 Begin in the first stitch next to the hook, and start by putting the hook under *both* strands of the "V" on the top of each stitch. Then continue with steps 2 and 3 for making a single crochet stitch. Repeat, single crocheting from right to left across the row.

Repeat steps 5, 6, and 7 until your swatch is as long as you want it to be.

8 At the end of your last row, cut the working yarn, leaving at least a 5-inch tail. Make a chain stitch, wrapping the cut tail around your hook from back to front, and pull it all the way through the loop on your hook. Pull tight on the tail to secure the knot.

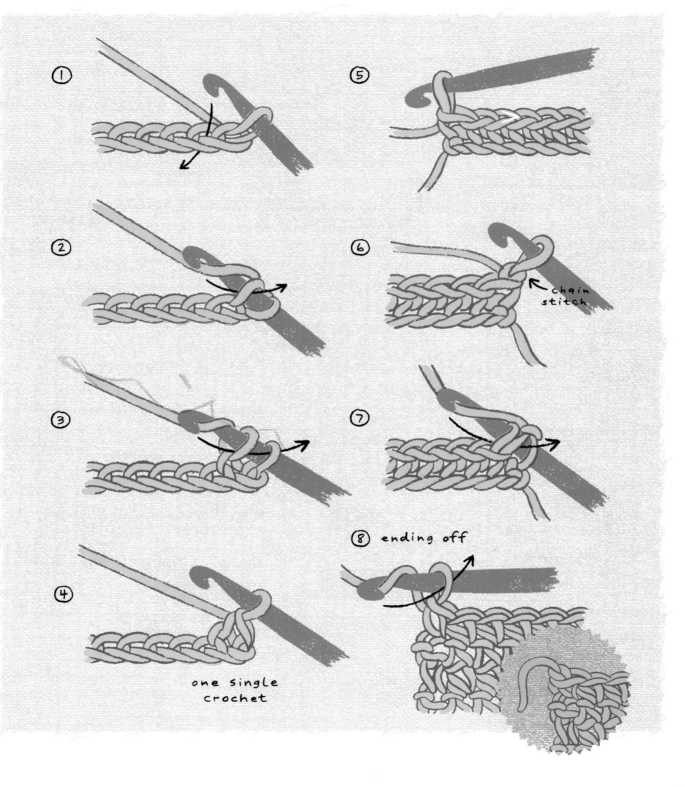

① ② ③ ④

one single
crochet

⑤ ⑥ chain
stitch

⑦ ⑧ ending off

Learning From Your Swatch

THIS MAY SEEM OBVIOUS BUT, AMAZINGLY, SOME PEOPLE FORGET TO LOOK AT WHAT THEY'RE CROCHETING CAREFULLY. THERE'S A LOT YOU CAN LEARN EVEN FROM THE SWATCH YOU MAKE WHEN YOU ARE LEARNING TO CROCHET.

what size is your swatch?

There are three things that will affect the size of your swatch: the thickness of your yarn, the size of your hook, and how loosely or tightly you make your single crochet stitches. If the stitches are very tight and you would like them to be looser, try using a larger hook. This will make the overall size of your swatch larger. If the stitches look very loose and you would like them to be tighter, try using a smaller hook. This will also make the overall size of your swatch smaller.

"right side" / "wrong side"

Each piece of crochet has a "right side" and a "wrong side." To determine which side is which, lay your piece down with the foundation row at the bottom, and the last row of single crochet stitches at the top. If the starting tail is coming out of the bottom left-hand corner of the piece, then the "right side" is facing up. If the starting tail is coming out of the bottom right-hand corner of the piece, then the "wrong side" is facing up.

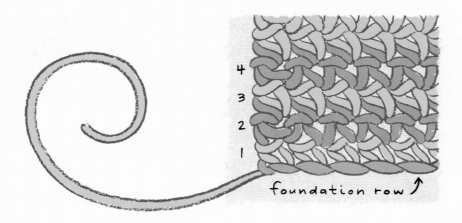

foundation row ↗

counting rows

To count the number of rows in your swatch, place it down on a flat surface, with the right side facing up, and count the rows on the right side of your work. At first, you might find it hard to see where each row begins and ends. Notice how the foundation row looks different from all the other rows, because it is made up of chain stitches. The rows of single crochet stitches also look slightly different from each other, and that is because you have turned your work at the end of each row. Notice how the stitches on row 3 go back to looking like those on row 1, and those on row 4 are just like those on row 2.

neck cozy

It won't take you any time at all to whip up one of these warm Neck Cozies. Working with a big size P hook and some super-bulky yarn makes the project easy to complete in an afternoon. The cozy is a perfect project to begin with, because it's nothing more than one extra-long swatch of single crochet. Unlike a long scarf, the cozy fastens around your neck with a button, slipped through a space between the stitches. Once you make one for yourself, you'll want to make more for friends and family.

1 To make a Neck Cozy that is approximately 5 inches wide, begin with a foundation row of 8 chain stitches (page 22).

2 Follow instructions for single crochet on page 24, and single crochet for about 38 more rows. *Remember to count your stitches at the end of each row. If you begin with 8 chain stitches, you should have 7 single crochet stitches in every row. Always turn the work from right to left at the end each row, and make one chain stitch before beginning the next row.*

materials

APPROXIMATELY 40 YARDS SUPER-BULKY YARN, SUCH AS CASCADE MAGNUM

1 SIZE P (11.5 MM) HOOK

YARN NEEDLE

1 LARGE BUTTON, APPROXIMATELY 1-INCH DIAMETER

STRONG SEWING OR EMBROIDERY THREAD AND A SEWING NEEDLE

3 Check to make sure your cozy will be long enough by wrapping it around your neck once. The ends should overlap in front of your neck by about 3 inches, making a V shape.

4 When you are happy with the length, end off (page 24), then weave in the tails with an oversized yarn needle (see near right).

5 Sew on a button (see far right) to one end of the cozy about 3 inches in from the bottom edge. Wrap the cozy around your neck and push the button through a space between the stitches to secure.

6 Once you have completed the cozy, lay it on a flat surface. Place a ruler or a tape measure over your work and count the number of single crochet stitches in a 4-inch-wide section. (Do not include the edge stitches in your measurement, and do not round off fractions.) This is called taking the gauge (gauge rhymes with *page*). The gauge of the neck cozy that Lola is wearing on page 29 is 6 stitches over 4 inches. What is the gauge of your neck cozy? Taking the gauge will become very important as you gain experience in crochet. For now, you're just doing it for practice.

Weaving in Tails

Most of the time you'll want to weave in any tails of yarn left hanging after you finish your work. There are two ways to weave in tails: down the side and inside the row. Either way, it's a good idea to weave in the tails through at least 6 stitches before snipping the end close to the work. Be careful not to cut your stitches!

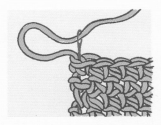

weaving tails down side
Weave them through the stitches on the side edges of your work.

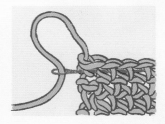

weaving tails inside row
Weave them through the inside of a row of single crochet stitches.

Sewing on a Button

It's important to sew your buttons onto your crochet securely so they won't fall off.

1 Choose a sewing needle and embroidery or sewing thread that will pass easily through the holes in your button. Thread the needle with about 10 inches of thread. Make 2 small stitches in the top of the crochet stitch at the spot where you want to place the button. This will secure the thread in place.

2 Poke the needle and thread up through 1 of the holes on the button (from the back to the front of the button). Now push the needle down into the next hole, through the crochet stitch underneath, and back up through the first hole again. Repeat this 4 or 5 times, and if there are 4 holes, do the same with the other 2. To finish, knot the thread under the button. Then run the needle through the inside of a few crochet stitches to hide the thread, and cut.

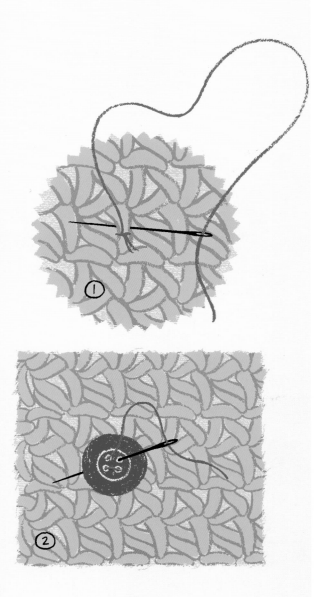

tool pouch

Transform a long rectangular swatch of single crochet into a useful pouch with a simple fold and a few whipstitches around the edges. Store crochet hooks, scissors, and a tape measure inside the pouch, and keep stitch markers and yarn needles handy by hooking them through the stitches on the front, under the flap.

crochet the body of the pouch

1 To make a pouch that is about 8 inches wide, begin with a foundation row of 23 chain stitches (page 22).

2 Follow directions for single crochet on page 24, and single crochet for about 48 rows, or until you have a rectangle that is 14 inches long. *Remember to count your stitches at the end of each row. If you begin with 23 chain stitches, you should have 22 single crochet stitches in every row. Always turn the work from right to left at the end of each row, and make 1 chain stitch before beginning the next row.*

materials

APPROXIMATELY 28 YARDS WORSTED-WEIGHT YARN IN ONE COLOR FOR THE POUCH, PLUS A FEW YARDS OF A SECOND COLOR TO SEW IT TOGETHER, SUCH AS WOOLY HILL FARM WORSTED

1 SIZE K (6.50 MM) HOOK

SPLIT-RING STITCH MARKERS

YARN NEEDLE

SMALL BUTTONS, APPROXIMATELY $\frac{1}{2}$-INCH DIAMETER

SEWING THREAD AND SEWING NEEDLE

3 When the rectangle is the right length, end off (page 24) and weave in the tails (page 30).

assemble the pouch

1 Block the rectangle so that it lays flat (see right) with the right side facing down (page 27). Bring the bottom up a little less than a third of the way to form the pocket, and leave a flap at the top that is about 5 inches long. Secure the side edges in place with a couple of stitch markers.

2 Thread a yarn needle with a contrasting color of yarn, then sew the edges together following the instructions for the whipstitch (see far right). Work from the bottom left-hand corner, stitching up the side towards the flap. When you get to the flap, continue stitching along its edge, then back down the other side.

3 Sew buttons on to the front of the pouch. For instructions on how to sew on a button see page 31. Make sure the buttons you choose are small enough to fit easily through the spaces between the crochet stitches, but large enough to hold the flap on the pouch closed.

Blocking

You may notice that your finished pieces of crochet don't always lay nice and flat, or keep the shape you intended. To solve this problem, you should always block individual pieces before sewing them together. The process of blocking will relax the stitches and make the piece of crochet softer. It will also give your project a more finished, professional look. There are a few different ways to block a piece of crochet. The simplest is the wet method. First, lay the piece of crochet on a clean bath towel with the right side facing down. Then smooth the edges out and pin them to the towel with straight pins so that the piece is the shape and size you want it to be. Now cover the entire piece with a damp dish towel and let it sit overnight, or until the dish towel and the piece of crochet are completely dry.

Whipstitch

Whipstitch is an easy way to assemble crocheted pieces. If you use the same yarn you used for the body of the project, the whipstitches won't be very obvious (but you will be able to see them). If you use a different color yarn, the whipstitches will be very obvious — in fact, they will become a nice decoration.

along side edges

Place wrong sides together, matching the rows. Thread a yarn needle with the same yarn you used for the piece, or with a contrasting color, and stitch the edges together, bringing the needle up, from back to front, in the spaces between each of the rows.

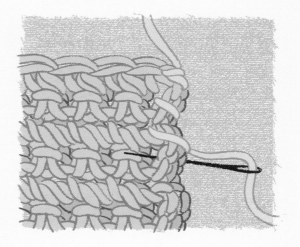

on top and bottom edges

Place the wrong sides together, lining up the stitches. Thread a yarn needle with the same yarn you used for the piece, or with a contrasting color, and stitch the edges together, bringing the needle up, from back to front, through both loops on the top of both of the stitches.

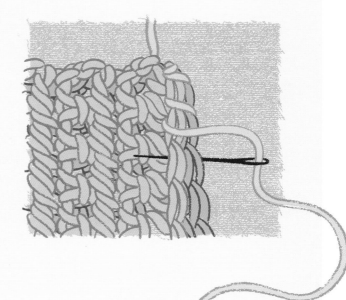

color

In this chapter, you'll learn to work
with two different-colored strands of yarn at
the same time to achieve a heathered effect.
You can also try switching from one color to another
on every row to produce a checked pattern,
or alternating colors on every two rows to
create even stripes. Or you can mix up the number
of rows between colors to see what other
patterns you can come up with.

When choosing colors for a project, look to
Mother Nature for good ideas. Notice how colors are
matched up on the wings of a butterfly, on the
scales of a fish, or on the petals of a flower.
The possibilities are endless.

Attaching a New Color

FOR THE PROJECTS IN THIS BOOK YOU WILL ALWAYS CHANGE COLORS AT THE BEGINNING OF A NEW ROW, AS SHOWN HERE.

1 Drop the working yarn at the end of the row, and let it fall to the back of the piece. Wrap the new color of yarn around the hook, and pull it through the loop on the hook.

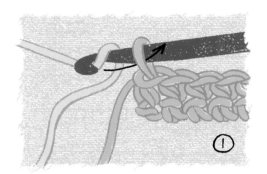

2 Pull down on the working yarn of the previous color to secure the new color of yarn.

3 Turn your work *from right to left*, and proceed with steps for single crochet (page 24) with the new color.

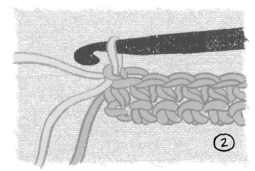

If you are going to continue single crocheting with this new color for a few rows, or if you are going to switch back and forth between 2 colors on every row, then cut the old color of yarn, leaving about a 6-inch tail so that you can weave it in later.

If you are going to make even stripes in repeating colors by switching colors every *other* row, then don't cut the old color of yarn. When you are ready to work with it again, carry it up the side of your piece and reattach it at the end of a row the same way you would a new color of yarn.

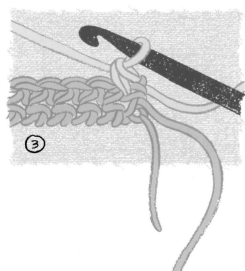

Color Effect

For fun, make lots of test swatches, changing how you work with the colors in each one. To keep the test swatches safe, stitch or glue them into a journal.

combining 2 different-colored strands of yarn to create a heathered effect

switching colors every row to create a checked pattern

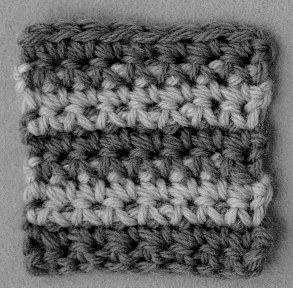

alternating colors on every 2 rows to create even stripes

mixing up the number of rows between colors

friendship cuffs

These colorful wrist cuffs are fun to make and trade with your friends, and they're a good way to try out different color combinations. Each cuff is one simple strip of single crochet, either sewn together at both ends, or secured with a button. You won't need a lot of yarn to make one cuff, so this is a perfect project for making use of leftover scraps of yarn from other projects. The cuffs Sofia is wearing in the photo at right were made with worsted yarn and a size J hook, but you can make them with just about any yarn. Remember that bulkier yarns usually require a larger hook, while lighter-weight yarns often work best with a smaller hook.

basic cuff

1 To make a basic cuff with the ends sewn together, start off with a foundation row of about 22 chain stitches (see page 22); the foundation row needs to be long enough to wrap loosely around your wrist once so that the first and last chains touch. If you make the foundation row too short, your finished cuff will end up being too small, and you won't be able to fit it over your hand. If you want to make a cuff that closes with a button, see page 42.

materials

ABOUT 10 YARDS WORSTED WEIGHT YARN, SUCH AS CASCADE 220 OR BROWN SHEEP NATURE SPUN, FOR 1 CUFF

1 SIZE J (6.00MM) HOOK

YARN NEEDLE

BUTTONS (OPTIONAL)

2 Once you have determined the right number of chain stitches to begin with, work in single crochet (see page 24) for 2 to 5 rows, or until the strip is the width you want your cuff to be. *Remember to count your stitches at the end of each row. For example, if you begin with a foundation row of 22 chain stitches, you should have 21 single crochet stitches in every row. Always turn the work from right to left at the end of each row, and make one chain stitch before beginning the next row.* For stripes, attach new colors of yarn at the end of each row. (To learn how to attach a new color, see page 38.)

3 End off, leaving a tail about 6 inches long to be used later on for sewing the ends together (see page 24). Weave any other leftover tails into the wrong side of the strip with a yarn needle (see page 30).

4 Block your strip of crochet to make it lay flat (see page 34). Then thread the leftover tail with a yarn needle and stitch the ends of the strip together with the woven stitch (see right). Make sure the right side (page 27) is on the outside of the cuff. After the last stitch, knot the yarn and weave the remainder of the tail into the wrong side of the cuff.

cuff with button

1 Begin as in step 1 of instructions for the basic cuff, making a foundation row of chain stitches you can wrap around your wrist once, but add about 2 more chain stitches, so that the first and last few chain stitches overlap.

2 Follow step 2 of the instructions for the basic cuff. Then end off (page 24), and weave in the tails (page 30).

3 Sew the button onto the right side of the strip, near the right-hand edge. (For instructions on how to sew on a button, see page 31.)

4 Wrap the crochet strip around your wrist and push the button through the space between a couple of the stitches on the other side of the strip. *When choosing a button for your cuff, keep in mind that it should be slightly larger than the spaces between your stitches, but not so big that it won't be able to pass through. If you want to use a larger button, try making the cuff with a larger hook, so that the spaces between your stitches will be wider.*

Woven Stitch

When you stitch together pieces of crochet using the woven stitch, your seams are invisible. You work the woven stitch slightly differently depending on whether you are attaching top and bottom edges or side edges, as shown here.

on top and bottom edges

Lay the pieces of crochet side by side, with right sides facing up, and line up the stitches of the top or bottom rows. Thread a yarn needle with the same yarn you used for the piece, and stitch the edges together as shown, bringing the needle up, from back to front, through the outer loops on the tops of the stiches.

along side edges

Sometimes you will need to attach your work along the side edges. To do this, lay the pieces side by side, with the right sides facing you, and line up the rows on each edge. Stitch the edges together as shown.

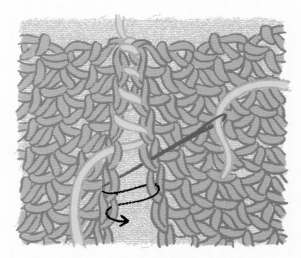

Woven Stitch on Top and Bottom Edges

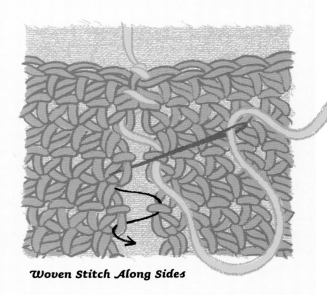

Woven Stitch Along Sides

43

striped bag

This simple Striped Bag offers yet another opportunity to play with different-colored yarns. There really is no limit to the combinations of stripes that you can dream up for your own unique design. Remember that you will need to single crochet for at least 2 rows with any one color in order to create a solid stripe. The body of the bag is one long rectangle of single crochet folded in half and sewn up along the side edges, and the strap is one long strip of single crochet attached to both sides. A felt liner secured to the inside with embroidery thread will keep small objects from slipping through the spaces between the stitches.

Materials

APPROXIMATELY 145 YARDS BULKY YARN, SUCH AS BROWN SHEEP LAMB'S PRIDE BULKY

SIZE L (8.0MM) CROCHET HOOK

YARN NEEDLE

ABOUT $\frac{1}{2}$ YARD FELT

1 SKEIN EMBROIDERY FLOSS

EMBROIDERY NEEDLE

make the body of bag

1 For a bag that is about 10 inches deep, start with a foundation row of 45 chain stitches (see page 22).

2 Follow instructions for single crochet on page 24, and single crochet for about 24 rows, or until the rectangle is about 9 inches wide. *Remember to count your stitches after each row. If you begin with 45 chain stitches, you should have 44 single crochet stitches in every row. Always turn the work from right to left at the end of each row, and make one chain stitch before beginning the next row. To make stripes of different colors follow directions for attaching a new color of yarn on page 38.*

3 When the rectangle is the right width, end off (page 24), and weave in the tails (page 30). This is the body of the bag.

4 Add a border of single crochet stitches around the rectangle (see page 46).

Crocheting a Border

Use these instructions to crochet a border around the Striped Bag or any other square or rectangular project.

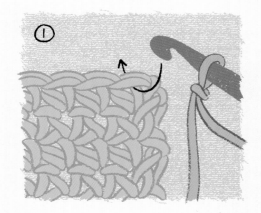

1 Make a slipknot and place it on your hook. Then put the hook through both loops of the corner stitch at the top right hand edge of your project, and proceed with steps for single crochet (page 24).

2 Make 2 more single crochet stitches in the same corner stitch, so that you have a total of 3 stitches in the same spot. Now continue adding a border of single crochet stitches all the way around the piece, always rounding the corners with 3 single crochet stitches in the same stitch. If you only make 1 single crochet stitch in the corners, they will curl up and your piece won't lay flat.

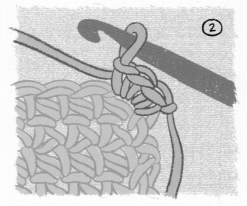

3 When you arrive back at the first corner, join the last stitch to the first stitch with a slip stitch: Put the tip of the hook through both loops on the top of the first stitch, wrap the working yarn around the hook, from back to front, and pull the hook all the way through all 3 of the loops on your hook. End off (page 24) and weave in tails (page 30).

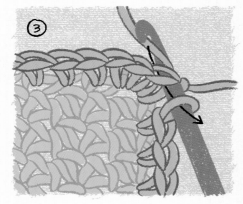

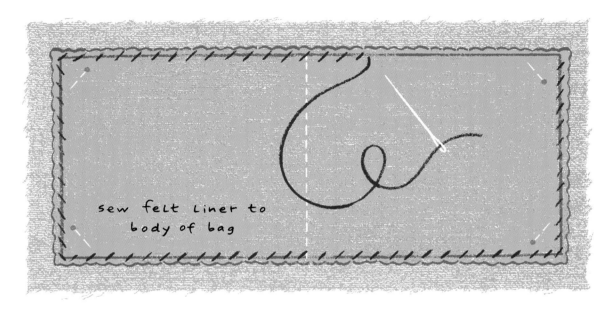

sew felt liner to body of bag

assemble the bag

1 Block the rectangle (body of bag) and strap so they lay nice and flat (see page 34). Lay the pieces on a clean, flat surface, such as a towel, with the wrong side facing you.

2 To make a liner for the bag, cut a piece of felt about $^1/_2$ inch smaller in length and width than the rectangle. Place the cut piece of felt in the center of the rectangle so that the edges of the felt are about $^1/_4$ inch inside the edges of the rectangle,

and hold the felt in place with straight pins. With an embroidery needle and embroidery thread, stitch the felt liner to the rectangle as shown above.

3 Fold the body of the bag in half (*see dotted line in illustration*), with the liner on the inside. Then thread a yarn needle with the same color yarn you used for the border, and sew the sides together following directions for whipstitch on page 35.

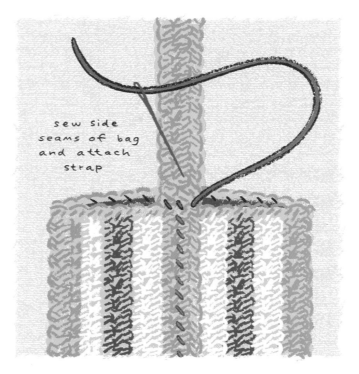

sew side
seams of bag
and attach
strap

make the strap

1 To make a strap that's about 35 inches long: leaving a 10–inch tail end, start with a foundation row of 74 chain stitches, and single crochet for 3 rows, or until the strap is about 2 inches wide. *Remember to count your stitches after each row. If you begin with 74 chain stitches, you should have 73 single crochet stitches in each row.* End off, leaving about a 10-inch tail.

2 Center the edges of the strap over the seams on either side of the bag, and hold in place with straight pins. With a yarn needle and the same yarn used to make the strap, attach the strap to the bag with stitches, as shown above, going back and forth a few times for strength.

Finding Crochet Help

When learning how to crochet, it's comforting to know someone with more experience who can answer your questions. Perhaps you have a parent or a sibling who knows how to crochet. If no one at home crochets, don't worry. People who love to crochet generally enjoy helping each other out, and with a little investigating, you're likely to find quite a few people who crochet right in your own neighborhood. Here are some ideas to get you started.

* Ask your family members if they know of anyone who crochets, such as a neighbor or friend.

* Ask the salespeople at your local yarn shop. They're often experienced at both knitting and crochet, and if they can't help you they're likely to know someone who can. Many yarn shops also offer classes on beginning and more advanced crochet techniques.

* Perhaps someone at school knows how to crochet, such as a teacher or a classmate, or someone at at a religious or other community center you attend.

* If you participate in an after-school program, such as dance or music lessons, or if you are a Girl Scout or Boy Scout, ask the instructors or troop leaders if they crochet.

* To find out if there is a crochet club in your area, contact the Crochet Guild of America (CGOA) either by writing to them at P.O. Box 3388 Zanesville, OH 43702, or by calling 704-452-4541. If you have access to the Internet, then look them up online at www.crochet.org. The website has a listing of "local chapters," which are basically crochet clubs that meet in different places. You can also contact the CGOA with questions about crochet either by phone at the toll-free number 877-852-9190 or via email at CGOA@crochet.org.

texture

You've learned how to **play with color.**
Now it's time to play with texture by learning
the rib stitch. The rib stitch is a variation on
the single crochet stitch done by working the stitches
through either the front loop or the back loop on the top of
each stitch. By crocheting through only one of the loops,
a ribbed texture forms. By combining these
stitches with the technique of attaching a new color
learned in the Color chapter, you can create a variety of
textures and patterns. Start off making a few sample
swatches to test out your new skills, and see what
unique combinations you can come up with.
Then sew them together to create the
Patchwork Poncho (page 58), or design your
very own Ribbed Scarf (page 54).

Rib Stitch

IN SINGLE CROCHET, YOU WORKED YOUR STITCHES BY PUTTING THE HOOK THROUGH BOTH LOOPS ON THE TOP OF THE STITCH. FOR THE RIB STITCH, YOU'LL WORK YOUR STITCHES BY PUTTING YOUR HOOK THROUGH ONLY ONE OF THESE LOOPS. YOU CAN CHOOSE BETWEEN THE FRONT LOOP OR THE BACK LOOP.

Begin by making a foundation row of chain stitches (page 22). Then start as you would for single crochet following the instructions on page 24, but when you get to Row 2, proceed as follows:

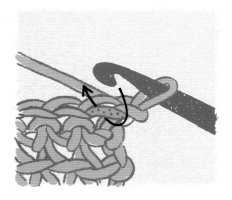

front loop

back loop

Put your hook through the front loop of the first stitch next to the hook and proceed with steps for making a single crochet stitch. Continue across the row, always putting your hook through the front loop of each stitch. Turn at the end of the row, make a chain stitch, and repeat.

Put your hook through the back loop of the first stitch next to the hook and proceed with steps for making a single crochet stitch. Continue across the row, always putting your hook through the back loop of each stitch. Turn at the end of the row, make a chain stitch, and repeat.

Front Loop

Back Loop

The front loop version of the rib stitch is a more elongated and flexible stitch than the regular crochet stitch and creates a fabric that hangs nicely, so it's a great stitch for making garments that hang, such as sweaters and scarves. The back loop version of the rib stitch creates a stretchy fabric with deep ridges.

ribbed scarf

What better way to practice combining the rib stitch (page 52) with color skills (page 38) than by making one long ribbed scarf. For this project you start with a long foundation row of chain stitches—166! Then you choose between one of the two versions of rib stitch, and start crocheting, switching colors on every row. When you finish crocheting you don't need to weave in any tails at the end, since the tails become part of the fringe!

materials

APPROXIMATELY 130 YARDS TOTAL WORSTED-WEIGHT YARN, SUCH AS CASCADE 220 (BETWEEN 25 AND 30 YARDS OF EACH COLOR, DEPENDING ON HOW MANY COLORS YOU CHOOSE TO WORK WITH, AND HOW WIDE YOU MAKE YOUR SCARF)

1 SIZE K (6.50 MM) CROCHET HOOK

1 To make a scarf that will be about 60 inches long, start with a foundation row of 166 chain stitches (see page 24 if you need help with your foundation row). Be sure to make your chain stitches nice and loose. If you lose track of how many chain stitches you've made, stop and count your stitches from the first chain you made up to the last one (to learn how to count chain stitches, see page 22), and then keep going.

2 Follow directions for single crochet on page 24, and crochet 1 row. *Remember to count your stitches at the end of the row. If you began with 166 chain stitches, you should now have 165 stitches in the row.*

3 Decide if you will make the remainder of your scarf by crocheting through either the front loop or the back loop of each stitch. To make a scarf with raised ribs, like the blue and green one, crochet through the back loop. For a scarf with flatter ribs, like the pink and brown one, crochet through the front loop.

Decisions, Decisions!

Which version of rib stitch will you choose? The blue and green scarf in the photograph was made with the BACK LOOP version, and the pink and brown scarf was made with the FRONT LOOP version.

4 Crochet for about 16 to 22 more rows, or until your scarf is the width you want it to be, switching to a new color of yarn at the end of each row. As you add and drop the different-colored yarns at the end of each row, cut the tails so that they are about 5 inches long. They're going to become part of the fringe you'll add on to the ends of the scarf later on, so you won't have to weave them in. When your scarf is the width you would like it to be, end off (see page 24).

5 Add fringe to both ends of the scarf following the instructions at right. If you like, match the color of your fringe to the rows of color in your scarf.

Adding Fringe

To make fringe for the Ribbed Scarf (or any other project), follow these instructions.

1 *Cut three 10-inch strands of yarn, and fold them in half to make a bundle of six 5-inch strands. Put the hook through the loop of the stitch at the top right-hand corner of the scarf. Catch the fold of the bundle of yarn with the tip of the hook, and pull the hook back down through the loop.*

2 *The bundle of strands should now be looped on the hook, so that there are 3 loops on the hook.*

3 *Now wrap all 6 of the ends of the bundle, plus—if you are making the Ribbed Scarf—the tail at the end of the row, around the hook, from back to front, and pull them down through all 3 of the loops on the hook. Keep pulling until the hook is released from the bundle.*

4 *Pull gently on the strands to secure the knot, and trim any uneven ends with scissors.*

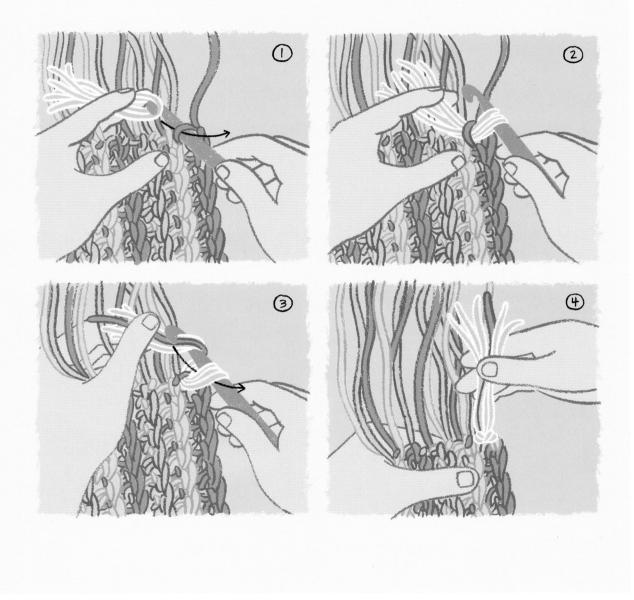

patchwork poncho

A collection of crochet squares that are the same in size can be sewn together to create a colorful patchwork poncho (or even a blanket). Practice all the skills learned up until now—single crochet, adding colors, rib stitch—and see how many different colorful combinations you can come up with! There's just one rule: Make sure all your swatches are the same size, otherwise you will have trouble sewing them together at the end. If you are making the poncho as shown in the photo, you will need to make thirty-six 4-inch squares. If you want to make your poncho smaller or larger, make your squares smaller or larger. Remember that not all yarns are the same, and you might need to switch hooks for certain yarns in order to keep your squares the same size.

materials

APPROXIMATELY 14 YARDS WORSTED-WEIGHT YARN FOR EACH SQUARE (APPROXIMATELY 504 YARDS TOTAL FOR PONCHO AS SHOWN)

1 SIZE J (6.00MM) CROCHET HOOK, OR WHATEVER SIZE HOOK IS NECESSARY TO ACHIEVE A 4-INCH SQUARE WITH YOUR YARN

YARN NEEDLE

measurements *(for poncho as shown)*

V-NECK TO BOTTOM CENTER POINT: 20 INCHES

ELBOW TO ELBOW: 27 $1/2$ INCHES

crochet the squares

The following instructions are for a 4-inch square made with a single strand of yarn.

1 Begin with a foundation row of 13 chain stitches (page 22).

2 Follow directions for single crochet on page 24, and single crochet for 3 rows. *Remember to count your stitches at the end of the row. If you began with 13 chain stitches, you should now have 12 stitches in the row.*

Always turn your work from right to left at the end of each row, and make one chain stitch before beginning the next row.

3 Pin the first 3 rows down to a flat surface, such as a towel, and lay a ruler or a tape measure across the width. If the measurement is more than 4 inches, start over with a hook that is one or two sizes smaller. If the measurement is less than 4 inches, try work-

ing with a hook that is one or two sizes larger. Continue testing the first 3 rows of the square until you achieve the 4-inch measurement.

4 Continue to single crochet for 10 to 12 more rows, or until the square measures 4 inches from top to bottom. End off and weave in tails.

Make 36 squares for the poncho.

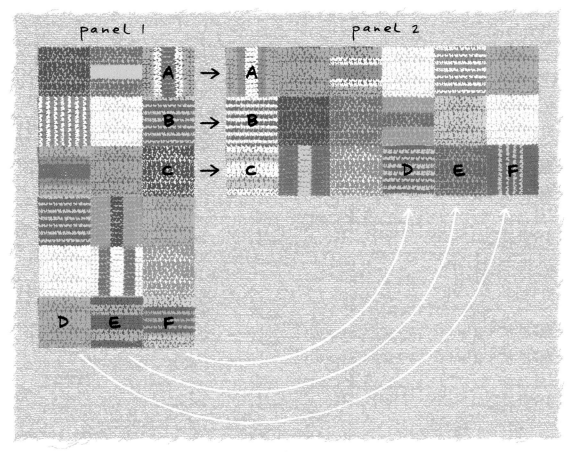

Assemble your poncho with a friend and you'll have it finished and ready to wear in no time.

all the squares are dry, unpin them, leaving them in position, and stitch the squares together with the woven stitch (page 43).

3 Attach panel 1 to panel 2, as shown in the diagram at left, with the woven stitch. Attach the sides labeled A, B, C first, and then join the sides labeled D, E, F.

assemble poncho

1 To make the first panel, lay half (18) of the squares, with their right sides facing up, on a flat, clean surface, such as a large towel. Arrange and pin them in 6 rows of 3 as shown in the diagram at left. As you pin the squares to the towel, line the edges and corners up, and block your squares altogether like this (for instructions on how to block, see page 34).

2 Repeat step 1 with the remaining 18 squares to create the second panel. When

crochet border around poncho

1 Add a border to the bottom edge of the poncho following the instructions on page 46. Add a double border around the neck edge by single crocheting for 2 rows, but don't make 3 single crochet stitches in the corners. When your borders are complete, end off, and weave in tails on the inside of the poncho.

2 Working in every other stitch, add fringe to the border along the bottom edge following the instructions on page 56.

shape

Up to this point, you have
learned to crochet shapes with straight edges,
such as the rectangle and the square, by single
crocheting the same number of stitches in every row.
To crochet a shape with angular edges,
like a triangle, oval, or diamond, you will need to
change the number of stitches that you single crochet
from row to row. This is called *increasing* (adding
stitches), and *decreasing* (subtracting
stitches). Once you learn these techniques,
spend some time experimenting to see what
shapes you can make by changing the number of
stitches from row to row.

Increasing and Decreasing

WHEN YOU "INCREASE," YOU ARE ADDING ONE MORE STITCH TO THE TOTAL
NUMBER OF STITCHES IN THE ROW THAT YOU ARE WORKING ON.
WHEN YOU "DECREASE," YOU ARE SUBTRACTING ONE STITCH FROM THE TOTAL
NUMBER OF STITCHES IN THE ROW THAT YOU ARE WORKING ON.

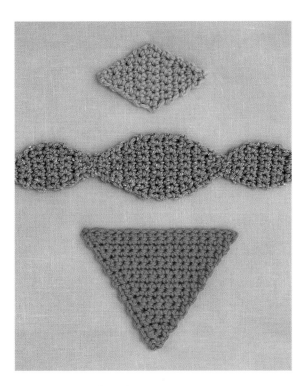

*Increase and/or decrease on every row
to create shapes with sharp, straight edges,
and on every other row to create more
gradual, rounded edges.*

increasing

1 Start by making one single crochet stitch
in the first stitch next to the hook (as shown
below). Then make another single crochet
stitch directly in the same stitch.

You have made one increase by making 2
single crochet stitches in the same stitch
(as shown in the illustration in the circle).

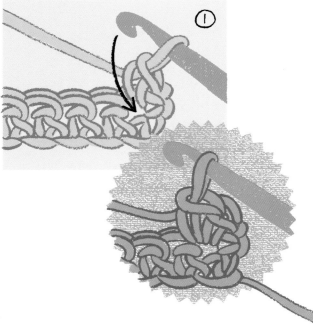

decreasing

1 To make a decrease, begin with steps for making the first half of a single crochet stitch: Put the hook through the first loop, then wrap the yarn around the hook from back to front and pull it back through the loop so that you have one loop on the hook. Now put the hook through the next stitch. Wrap the yarn around the hook from back to front again, and pull it back through the loop, so that you end up with 3 loops on the hook.

2 Wrap the yarn around the hook one more time, and pull it through all 3 loops on your hook.

You have made one *decrease* by single crocheting two stitches together to make one stitch (as shown in the illustration in the circle).

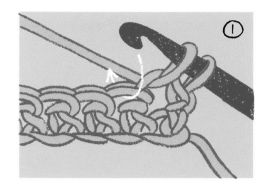

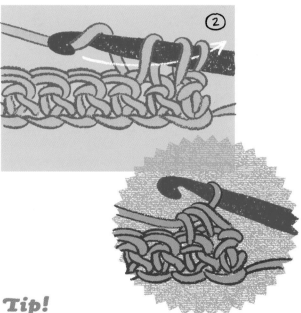

Tip!

Most of the increases and decreases in the patterns in this book are made at the beginning and/or end of a row, but increasing can also occur in the middle of a row.

wavy headband

This headband begins and ends with a chain so that you can tie it easily around your head. It's made of five oval shapes, each made with a series of increases and decreases so it ends up looking wavy. Follow the pattern below to make a headband like the one Isabelle is wearing, or experiment with your own combinations of increases and decreases and design your own version.

materials

APPROXIMATELY 25 YARDS WORSTED-WEIGHT YARN, SUCH AS TAHKI NEW TWEED

SIZE H (5.00 MM) CROCHET HOOK

YARN NEEDLE

start the first oval

1 Begin with a foundation row of 36 chain stitches (page 24). Skip over the first chain stitch next to the hook, and make an increase by making 2 single crochet stitches in the second chain stitch from the hook (see page 64). You will have a total of 2 single crochet stitches.

2 Turn the row of 2 stitches from right to left and make a chain stitch to begin the next row, then single crochet for 1 row. (*Remember to always turn your work and make a chain stitch at the end of each row.*)

3 On the next row, make an increase in the first stitch, and then make another increase in the second stitch so that you have a total of 4 stitches.

4 Single crochet for the next 3 rows.

5 Make a *decrease* by single crocheting the first 2 stitches together (see page 65) at the beginning of the next row, and then joining the last 2 stitches together at the end of the row. You will now have a total of 2 stitches.

6 Single crochet for 1 row.

start the second oval

1 Repeat step 3 of instructions for the first oval.

2 Single crochet for 1 row.

3 Make an *increase* at the beginning and end of the next row, so that you have a total of 6 stitches.

4 Single crochet for 5 rows.

5 Make a *decrease* at the beginning and end of the next row, so that you have a total of 4 stitches.

6 Single crochet for 1 row.

7 Repeat step 5 and 6 of instructions for the first oval.

start the third oval

1 Repeat steps 1 through 3 of instructions for the second oval.

2 Single crochet for 1 row.

3 Make an *increase* at the beginning and end of the next row, so that you have a total of 8 stitches.

4 Single crochet for 7 rows.

5 Make a *decrease* at the beginning and end of the next row, so that you have a total of 6 stitches.

6 Single crochet for 1 row.

7 Repeat steps 5 through 7 of instructions for the second oval.

for the fourth oval
Repeat instructions for making the second oval.

for the fifth oval
Repeat steps 2 through 6 of instructions for the first oval.

to finish,
decrease the last 2 stitches together, so that you have 1 stitch. Then make 35 chain stitches, end off, and weave the tails into the chains (page 30).

Become a "Crocheteer"

Volunteering your time and talents to help someone who is struggling is the perfect way to have fun while truly making a difference. Across the nation, kids and adults are doing just this by crocheting blankets, caps, mittens, socks, scarves, and sweaters for sick and orphaned children, soldiers overseas, and people who have lost their homes or loved ones. To become a "crocheteer," create items for people in need right in your neighborhood, or sign up with one of the many organizations that help distribute items around the world. Below are a few organizations that can help you get started.

Caps for Kids (administered by the Craft Yarn Council of America)
Collects and distributes caps.

Warm up America (administered by the Craft Yarn Council of America)
Collects and stitches together afghan squares, then distributes the afghans.

Craft Yarn Council of America
P.O. Box 9
Gastonia, NC 28053-0009
Phone: 704-824-7838 or 800-662-9999
www.craftyarncouncil.com/caps.html
www.warmupamerica.com

Project Linus
Collects and distributes blankets for children.
P.O. Box 5621
Bloomington, IL 61702-5621
Phone: 309-664-7814
www.projectlinus.org

Crochet Guild of America
Maintains a long list of charities that accept handmade donations.
P.O. Box 3388
Zanesville, OH 43702
Tel: 740-452-4541
www.crochet.org/charity2.html

triangle-square
quilt & pillow

Did you know that by putting two triangles together it's possible to make one square? That's exactly what a triangle-square is. Even better is the fact that by sewing these triangle-squares together it's possible to make even larger squares, which can then be sewn together to make one giant square. Lots of designs can be created with these triangle-squares, depending on the colors you choose and how you decide to arrange the squares before sewing them together. One way to arrange them is by "motifs." A motif is a single unit, in this case made up of a number of squares sewn together, that is repeated several times to create a pattern.

This type of project takes some time to complete, but it's easy to manage if you just think about doing one square at a time.

materials

WORSTED-WEIGHT YARN (SUCH AS BROWN SHEEP NATURE SPUN OR LAMB'S PRIDE SUPERWASH) AS FOLLOWS FOR EACH PROJECT AS SHOWN:

for the quilt: ONE TRIANGLE-SQUARE REQUIRES APPROXIMATELY 38 YARDS, SO YOU WILL NEED ABOUT 2,432 YARDS OF ALL COLORS COMBINED TO MAKE THE WHOLE QUILT, AND ANOTHER 100 YARDS FOR THE BORDER.

for the pillow: ONE TRIANGLE-SQUARE REQUIRES APPROXIMATELY 26 YARDS, SO YOU WILL NEED ABOUT 416 YARDS OF ALL COLORS COMBINED TO MAKE THE FRONT OF THE PILLOW, AND ANOTHER 360 YARDS TO MAKE THE BACK.

SIZE H (5.00 MM) HOOK

YARN NEEDLE

20-INCH PILLOW FORM, IF YOU ARE MAKING A PILLOW LIKE THE ONE SHOWN AT THE RIGHT

measurements

quilt: APPROXIMATELY 50 INCHES SQUARE

pillow: EXACTLY 20 INCHES SQUARE

plan your project

1 First, decide if you will make a pillow (5-inch squares) or a quilt (6-inch squares). Then decide if you will make your project exactly like the ones in the photographs, or if you will create your own design. To make the projects as they appear here, follow the diagrams on pages 76 and 78. If you are planning your own design, draw out the pattern ahead of time on graph paper with colored pencils. You can create a "crazy-quilt" pattern like the one Chelsea is planning above, or for a less wild look, you can use the diagrams on the following pages for inspiration, and design one motif made up of several squares first and then repeat it.

2 Decide what colors of yarn you want to use to make your project. Unless you have a lot of scrap yarn leftover from other projects, try to limit your choice to five colors or fewer.

3 Use your design to figure out how much of each color of yarn you are going to need to complete your project. Each individual triangle requires approximately 19 yards of worsted-weight yarn, so to figure out how many yards of yarn you will need of a certain color in your design, count out the total number of triangles you have drawn in that color and then multiply that number by 19. Repeat for each color in your design. *If you are making the pillow, remember to add about 360 yards to make the back piece, and if you are making the quilt, include about 100 yards to make the border.*

start following the pattern

The following pattern includes 2 sets of numbers. The first set of numbers is for the 6-inch squares for the quilt. The numbers in parentheses are for the 5-inch squares for the pillow. For example, in Step 1 you begin with 33 chain stitches if you are making the quilt and 25 chain stitches if you are making the pillow. If you like, to make it easier to keep track of what you are doing, before you start crocheting, read through the pattern and highlight all of the numbers for the size/project you are working on.

make the first half of the triangle-square

1 Begin with a foundation row of 33 (25) chain stitches (page 22).

2 Follow directions on page 24 for single crochet, and single crochet for 1 row. *Remember to count your stitches at the end of the row. If you began with 33 (25) chain stitches, you should now have 32 (24) stitches in the row. Always turn the work from right to left at the end of each row, and make one chain stitch before beginning the next row.*

3 Make a decrease, by single crocheting 2 stitches together (page 65), once at the beginning and once again at the end of the next row. Then count your stitches — you should have 2 stitches fewer than you began with. If you had 32 (24) stitches in the previous row, you should now have 30 (22) stitches in this row.

4 Repeat step 3, making a decrease at the beginning and end of each row, for 13 (10) more rows (that means 16 (13) rows total).

This means you will be decreasing 2 stitches on each row. Follow the chart below to help keep track of how many stitches you should have at the end of each row. Use a pencil to check off each row as you complete it. *At this point, you should be at row 3.*

Row	Quilt	Pillow
foundation	33	25
1	32	24
2	30	22
3	**28**	**20**
4	**24**	**18**
5	**22**	**16**
6	**20**	**14**
7	**18**	**12**
8	**16**	**10**
9	**14**	**8**
10	**12**	**6**
11	**10**	**4**
12	**8**	**2**
13	**6**	**1**
14	**4**	
15	**2**	
16	**1**	

5 After finishing row 15 (12), when there are 2 stitches left, decrease them together so that you end up with 1 stitch. End off (page 24) and weave in the tails (page 30).

6 Check your gauge following the instructions on the next page. Once you know you are crocheting at the correct gauge, make the second half of the triangle-square.

make the second half of the triangle-square

1 Make a slipknot with the new color of yarn and put it on your hook (see top illustration at right). Then hold the first triangle with the right side facing you and the foundation row at the top, so that the very first chain stitch you made is in the upper right hand corner. Now put the hook through the top loop of the first chain stitch in the foundation row, and proceed with steps for single crochet (see bottom illustration at right). Continue, making single crochet stitches across the foundation row. This row of single crochet stitches is considered the foundation row of the second triangle, and it should have 32 (24) stitches.

2 Turn the work from right to left and make 1 chain stitch (remember to do this at the end of each row). Single crochet for 1 row in each of the stitches, without decreasing.

3 At *this point, you are at the beginning of row 2*. Now begin making a decrease (page 65) at the beginning and end of each row for the remaining rows. Follow the same chart you followed for the first triangle to help keep track of what row you are on.

4 On the last row (row 15 (12)), when there are 2 stitches left, decrease them together so that you end up with 1 stitch. End off and weave in the tails.

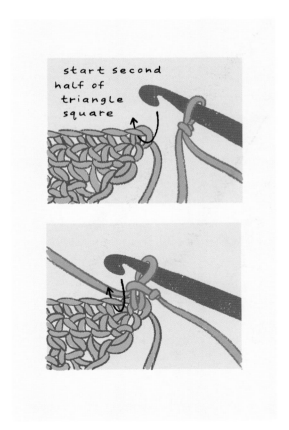

start second half of triangle square

Checking Gauge

In crochet, the number of rows you work per inch is referred to as the gauge (rhymes with "page"). For this project, you should be crocheting 14 stitches over 4 inches. If you are making the blanket and your gauge is a little off, your results will probably be fine (however, if you are crocheting a lot looser than recommended you will need extra yarn). But, if you are making the pillow, you really need to crochet at the correct gauge so that it will fit on the pillow form. To test your gauge, practice crocheting the first half of a triangle-square following the directions on page 74, then pin it down on a flat surface, such as a towel, and measure over a 4-inch-wide section with a ruler or tape measure. If the number of stitches over 4 inches is fewer than 14, switch to working with a hook that is one size larger. If the number of stitches is more than 14, switch to working with a hook that is one size smaller. Continue practicing the first half of a triangle square until you reach the correct gauge.

Triangle-Square Quilt

To make a quilt exactly like the one shown on page 72, assemble the pieces as shown here.

assemble the quilt

The quilt pictured on page 72 is approximately 50-inches square, including the border, and is made out of sixty-four 6-inch squares. It's made of 4 motifs, and each motif is made up of 16 triangle-squares: 8 blue and pink, and 8 brown and pink.

1 Begin working one motif at a time. Arrange the squares according to the design you want to achieve, with the right sides facing down, on a flat, clean surface, such as a large towel. Pin the squares to the towel, lining up the edges and corners. Block your squares all together like this (see blocking instructions on page 34).

2 When the squares are dry, unpin them and leave them in position. Then attach them at each point where 4 corners meet:

STEP A: Thread a yarn needle with a 10-inch strand of the same yarn you used to make the squares, and attach it to corner A with a couple of stitches, leaving about a 5-inch tail. Then work counterclockwise, threading the yarn through the corner on each triangle. Follow from point A to point B, and continue all the way to point H as shown at right.

STEP B: Remove the needle, and pull gently on the yarn tail, drawing all the corners in towards each other, keeping the center point flat. Tie the 2 yarn tails together in a tight double knot, and weave in the tails on the wrong side.

3 Once all the corners are attached, turn the squares over so that the right sides are facing you, and stitch all the sides of the squares together with the woven stitch (page 43). Repeat for each motif.

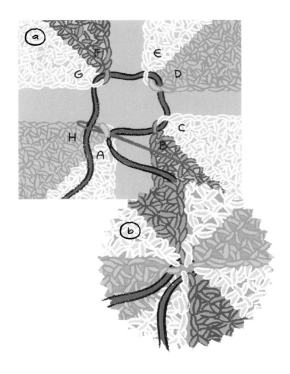

4 Once all 4 motifs are assembled, lay all 4 motifs out. Repeat the directions in step 2 for sewing them all together.

5 To finish, add a border of 3 rows of single crochet stitches around the entire edge of the quilt. You can crochet all 3 rows in the same color yarn, or switch to a different color for each row (see instructions on page 46 if you need help making the border).

Triangle-Square Pillow

To make a pillow exactly like the one shown on page 71, assemble the pieces as shown here.

assemble the pillow

The pillow pictured on page 71 is a 20-inch square, and has twenty-four $4^1/_2$-inch squares in it. It's made of 4 motifs, and each motif is made up of 4 squares: 2 red and white, and 2 orange and white.

1 To assemble your pillow, follow steps 1 through 4 of the instructions for assembling the quilt.

2 Make a 20-inch square of single crochet for the back of pillow. Begin with a foundation row of 71 chain stitches, and crochet for about 90 rows (70 single crochet stitches in each row), or until the square measures 20 inches from top to bottom. End off and weave in tails.

3 To attach the pillow back to the front piece, put the wrong sides together, and with a strand of the same yarn and a yarn needle, stitch along 3 sides with the woven stitch. Stuff with a 20-inch pillow form, and then stitch the remaining side shut. Weave the tails in through seam to the inside of the pillow.

Start a Crochet Club

One of the best parts of crocheting is sharing what you learn and what you make with your friends. Why not start an after-school or week-end crochet club? You and your buddies can have fun getting together to work on your latest crochet projects, while sharing ideas for new projects, and helping each other get past tricky spots. For extra fun, ask each member to make swatches to trade, then help each other sew the squares together to make friendship blankets!

circular
crochet

Get ready to learn how to crochet a circle!
All you need to know is how to single crochet (page 24),
and how to increase (page 64). The main difference
between circular and regular crochet is that in regular
crochet you work back and forth in rows and turn
the piece over at the end of each row, but in circular
crochet you crochet around and around on the
same side without turning. Circular crochet—also
known as crochet in the round—can be used to make
objects out of flat circular shapes like the colorful Critter
Cushions Taia is making at right, or to make tubular
objects like the hats featured on page 95.

Circular Crochet

THERE ARE SEVERAL WAYS TO BEGIN A CIRCLE IN CROCHET.
THE FOLLOWING STEPS SHOW YOU HOW TO MAKE THE FIRST THREE
ROUNDS OF A BASIC CIRCLE WITH A TIGHT CENTER.

1 Begin with a foundation row of 2 chain stitches (see page 22). Skip over the first chain stitch next to the hook and put your hook through the second chain stitch. Continue with steps for making a single crochet stitch (see page 24).

2 Make 5 more single crochet stitches into the same chain stitch until you have a total of 6 stitches. As you make the second stitch, move the tail over to the right side of the hook, so that the slipknot gets caught under the working yarn as you wrap it from front to back. After each stitch, pull on the tail a little to keep the center from opening up too much. When you've completed 6 stitches, hold the center of the circle in between your thumb and index finger, and pull the tail firmly to tighten the center. *If you have trouble tightening the center, start over from the beginning and make sure the slipknot gets caught under the stitches by the second or third stitch.*

3 Before beginning the next round, place a split-ring stitch marker or safety pin in the last stitch of the previous round. Pass the pointed end of the marker through the 2 loops on the front of the stitch. *Moving the marker to the last stitch at the end of each round will help you keep track of where each new round should begin and end.* Now put your hook under both loops on the top of the first stitch of round 1, and proceed with steps for making a single crochet stitch.

4 Increase 1 by making another single crochet stitch in the same stitch (see page 64). You should now have 2 single crochet stitches in the same stitch.

5 Continue, making an increase in each of the remaining 5 stitches in the first round, until you have a total of 12 stitches. *Remember to always move the marker to the last stitch of each round.*

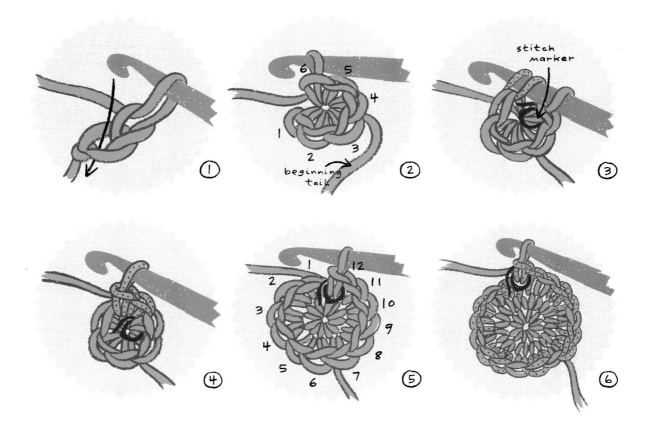

stitch marker

① ② ③

④ ⑤ ⑥

6 in image 2 labels: 6 5 4 1 2 3 beginning tail

image 5 labels: 1 2 12 3 11 4 10 9 5 8 6 7

6 For the third round, make an increase in every *other* stitch. To do this, *single crochet once in the first stitch and then make an increase by making 2 single crochet stitches in the next stitch.* Repeat the instruction in between the *asterisks* 5 more times. This will bring you to the end of the round, and you will have a total of 18 stitches.

Now you know how to get a circle started in single crochet. If you want to make your circle even bigger, continue making rounds of single crochet stitches, and with each round add 1 to the total number of stitches that you make before increasing. For example, on the next round make an increase in every third stitch, and on the next, make one in every fourth stitch, and so on. To end off or attach a new color, see pages 84–85.

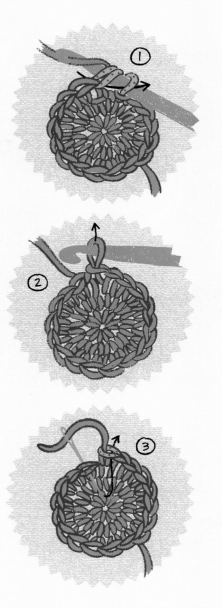

ending off in circular crochet

To finish the crocheted circle so that it will not unravel, follow these instructions:

1 On the last round of your circle, join the last stitch to the first stitch with a slip stitch: Put the tip of the hook through both loops on the top of the first stitch, then wrap the working yarn around the hook, from back to front, and pull the hook through all 3 of the loops on your hook.

2 Cut the working yarn, leaving about a 5-inch long tail, and pull it up and out of the stitch. Do not make a knot.

3 Thread the tail onto a yarn needle and draw it through both loops of the next stitch, from back to front, and then back through both loops of the last stitch, from front to back. Turn the circle over and weave the tail through the stitches on the back.

There are several methods for switching colors and attaching a new strand of yarn in circular crochet. The following method will allow you to switch colors midway through a single crochet stitch without creating what is called "color drag." This happens when you try to attach the yarn at the beginning of a single crochet stitch and you end up with a tiny stitch of the old color in the stripe of the new color.

1 On the last single crochet stitch of a round, stop midway through the stitch at the point where there are 2 loops on the hook. Then let the working yarn drop to the back of the circle, and pick up a strand of the new color of yarn. Wrap it around the hook, and pull it down through the 2 loops on the hook.

2 You now have one loop of the new color of yarn on the hook, and you are ready to begin the next round.

3 Complete one round of single crochet with the new color, and then join the first and last stitches of the round together with a slipstitch (see step 1 of ending off).

Continue crocheting with the new color of yarn for as many rounds as you like. *Do not make a slipstitch at the end of each subsequent round.*

When you are ready to switch colors again, either repeat steps 1–3 with a new color of yarn, or with the color of yarn that you let drop earlier (as long as you haven't crocheted more than 4 rounds since dropping it). To do this, simply carry it up along the wrong side of the circle and attach it the same way you would a new color of yarn, following steps 1–3. Remember to leave about a 5-inch tail when you cut the yarn.

To make single rings of color, you will need to switch from one color of yarn to another immediately after completing just one round of a color. To do this, attach the new color as you make the slipstitch at the end of the round.

critter cushions

These colorful cushions are made of 2 large crochet circles sewn together around a pillow form. The following pattern is for cushions in three different standard sizes: 10-inch, 12-inch and 14-inch. For all 3 sizes, you'll start off crocheting a circle for 6 rounds, increasing on every round. Then, to make the edges of each circle curve in on the sides, you'll switch to increasing on every other round for the remainder of the pattern. The butterfly and snail appliqués are made of separate crochet circles that are sewn on at the end.

materials

BULKY-WEIGHT YARN, SUCH AS CRYSTAL PALACE ICELAND. APPROXIMATELY 172 YARDS FOR THE LARGE CUSHION, 132 YARDS FOR THE MEDIUM, AND 98 YARDS FOR THE SMALL.

SIZE K (6.50MM) CROCHET HOOK

1 PILLOW FORM FOR EACH CUSHION: 10-INCH FOR THE SMALL CUSHION, 12-INCH FOR THE MEDIUM CUSHION, AND 14-INCH FOR THE LARGE CUSHION, OR ONE BAG OF COTTON OR POLY-ESTER FIBER STUFFING FOR EACH CUSHION.

SPLIT-RING STITCH MARKERS OR SAFETY PINS

YARN NEEDLE

BUTTONS OR BEADS, FOR SNAIL'S EYES (OPTIONAL)

measurements

SMALL CUSHION: 15 ROUNDS = 10"

MEDIUM CUSHION: 19 ROUNDS = 12"

LARGE CUSHION: 21 ROUNDS = 14"

gauge

THE FIRST 3 ROUNDS OF THE PATTERN = 2 INCHES

The instructions here are for cushions made in a single color of yarn. If you are making a cushion with rings of color, switch colors at the end of a round (see page 85 for instructions on how to attach a new color in circular crochet).

for all three cushion sizes

Follow steps 1 through 6 of instructions on pages 82–83 for getting the first three rounds of a circle started. Make sure you have a total of 18 stitches at the end of the third round. Then check to make sure your gauge is correct for this pattern (see instructions at right), and move the marker to the last stitch. *Remember, at the end of each new round, count the total number of stitches, and then move the marker to the last stitch.*

Round 4 *Single crochet in the next 2 stitches, and then make an increase by making 2 single crochet stitches in the 3rd stitch (if you need help increasing, see page 64).* Repeat the instruction between the asterisks 5 more times. This will bring you to the end of the round, and you will have a total of 24 stitches.

Measuring Gauge in Circular Crochet

Whenever you are following a pattern in circular crochet, it's a good idea to measure your gauge (the number of rounds per inch) after completing the first 3 rounds. This way, you will know right away if you are using the right size hook to get the gauge you need or if you need to try a different hook size. After completing the first 3 rounds, lay a ruler or tape measure across the center of the circle from one edge to the other. If the first 3 rounds equal less than the desired gauge, try working with a slightly larger hook, and if they equal more, then try working with one that is slightly smaller.

Round 5 *Single crochet in the next 3 stitches, then make an increase in the 4th stitch.* Repeat the instruction between the asterisks 5 more times, which will bring you to the end of the round, and you will have a total of 30 stitches.

Round 6 *Single crochet in the next 4 stitches, then make an increase in the 5th stitch.* Repeat the instruction between the asterisks 5 more times, which will bring you to the end of the round, and you will have a total of 36 stitches.

Round 7 Single crochet for one complete round without making any increases.

Round 8 *Single crochet in the next 5 stitches, then make an increase in the 6th stitch.* Repeat the instruction between the asterisks 5 more times, which will bring you to the end of the round, and you will have a total of 42 stitches.

Round 9 Single crochet for one complete round without making any increases

Round 10 *Single crochet in the next 6 stitches, then make an increase in the 7th stitch.* Repeat the instruction between the

asterisks 5 more times, until you end up with a total of 48 stitches. Continue to work, increasing for every round, adding 1 to the number of single crochet stitches you make before increasing.

For the small cushion Do this for 4 more rounds until you have a total of 60 single crochet stitches. Then single crochet for 1 more round without making any increases, and end off (page 84). You will have completed a total of 15 rounds.

For the medium cushion Do this for 8 more rounds, until you have a total of 72 single crochet stitches, and end off (page 84). You will have completed a total of 19 rounds.

For the large cushion Do this for 10 more rounds, until you have at total of 78 single crochet stitches. Then single crochet for 1 more round without making any increases, and end off (page 84). You will have completed a total of 21 rounds.

Repeat the instructions from the beginning to make a second circle the same size as the first (one circle is the front of the cushion and one circle is the back of the cushion).

Keeping Track of Your Rounds

In circular crochet, it's easy to lose track of which round you're working on. Counting the number of stitches at the end of each round helps on rounds when you are increasing stitches, but once you begin making continuous rounds of the same number of stitches, you'll need another way to keep from getting lost. The simplest way is to make a list of the total number of rounds in the pattern, and then check off the number for each round as you complete it.

In this swatch, 8 rounds of circular crochet have been worked.

assemble the cushions

Place the 2 circles on either side of the pillow form, so that the right sides are facing out. Flatten the centers of the circles over the pillow form, and spread the edges out. Line up the stitches along the outer edges of both circles and secure the circles to each other (with the pillow form in the center) using split-ring markers or safety pins. Using the same yarn you used to crochet and a yarn needle, sew the circles together with the woven stitch (see page 43 if you need help with the woven stitch). *If you are using stuffing instead of a pillow form, then sew your circles together leaving about a 5-inch opening, and fill them with the stuffing before sewing the opening shut.* If desired, crochet a butterfly or snail to decorate the pillow, as follows:

make the butterfly

1 To make the body, begin with a foundation row of 10 chain stitches, and crochet 9 single crochet stitches for 1 row. End off, and cut the beginning and ending tails about 1 $^{1}/_{2}$ inches long. Knot the ends of the tails to make them look like antennae.

2 Each of the butterfly's lower wings is simply 2 rounds of circular crochet, and each of the upper wings is 3 rounds. Follow the directions on page 82 for getting a circle started up to round 2 for the lower wings, and up to round 3 for the upper wings. Make two of each. Use a yarn needle and the leftover tails to sew them to either side of the body with the woven stitch.

3 Sew the butterfly's body to the center of the pillow with the woven stitch, and make a few stitches around the edges of the wings. Secure the antennae in place by making a tiny stitch through the back of each knot at the tip of the tails.

make the snail

1 To make the body, begin with a foundation row of 23 chain stitches and then crochet 22 single crochet stitches for 1 row. End off, and cut the beginning and ending tails about 1 $^{1}/_{2}$ inches long. Knot the ends of the tails to make them look like the antennae.

2 To make the shell, follow directions for making the small pillow up to round 6, changing colors whenever you want, and then single crochet for one more round without making any increases.

3 Use a yarn needle and some of the same yarn to sew the body to the center of the pillow with the woven stitch. Then stuff the shell with some leftover scraps of yarn and sew it over the body onto the pillow, so that its head and tail are peeking out on either side. Secure the antennae in place by making a tiny stitch through the back of each knot at the tip of the tails. Stitch on tiny buttons or beads for eyes with a regular sewing needle and thread.

hat trick

This snug hat, made with bulky yarn, will keep your head nice and warm on frosty winter days. It's so quick and easy to crochet and can be made to look different so easily by adding small details like a flat or pointy top or earflaps, ties, or fringe, that you'll probably want to make one for each of your friends.

For this project you will need to match the gauge—3 rounds = 3 inches—so that the hat fits snugly.

The following pattern is for making a hat out of a single color of yarn. If you want to make a striped hat, switch colors at the end of a round (see page 85 for instructions on adding a new color).

materials *(for one hat)*

APPROXIMATELY 100 YARDS BULKY-WEIGHT YARN FOR THE BASIC HAT. TO MAKE A HAT WITH EARFLAPS AND TASSEL TIES, YOU WILL NEED AN ADDITIONAL 10 YARDS. HATS SHOWN IN BROWN SHEEP LAMB'S PRIDE BULKY, REYNOLDS BULKY LOPI, AND MOREHOUSE FARM MERINO.

SIZE N (10MM) CROCHET HOOK

YARN NEEDLE

CARDBOARD, FOR MAKING TASSELS (OPTIONAL) – APPROXIMATELY 2 INCHES WIDE X 4–5 INCHES LONG

BUTTONS (OPTIONAL)—AS MANY OR AS FEW AS YOU WANT FOR DECORATION

gauge

THE FIRST 3 ROUNDS OF THE PATTERN = 3 INCHES

to make hat with flat top

Follow steps 1 through 6 of instructions on 82–83 for getting the first 3 rounds of a circle started. Make sure you have a total of 18 stitches at the end of the third round. Then check to make sure your gauge is correct for this pattern (page 88), and move the marker to the last stitch. *Remember, at the end of each new round, count the total number of stitches, then move the marker to the last stitch.*

Round 4 *Single crochet in the next 2 stitches, then make an increase by making 2 single crochet stitches in the 3rd stitch (page 64).* Repeat the instruction between the asterisks 5 more times, which will bring you to the end of the round; you will have a total of 24 stitches.

Round 5 *Single crochet in the next 3 stitches, then make an increase in the 4th stitch.* Repeat the instruction between the asterisks 5 more times, which will bring you to the end of the round; you will have a total of 30 stitches.

Continue to work, increasing on *every* round, adding 1 to the number of single crochet stitches you make before increasing. Do this for 2 more rounds until you have a total of 42 single crochet stitches.

make the body of the hat

If you want to make a hat without any earflaps, single crochet around without making any increases for 15 more rounds, then end off (page 84). *To help keep track of what round you are on as you work, write down the numbers 1 through 15 on a piece of paper, and check off the number for each round as you complete it.*

If you want to make a hat with earflaps, single crochet around without making any increases for 11 more rounds, then move the marker to the last stitch of the last round.

to make the earflaps

Begin working in rows.

Row 1 Single crochet in the next 8 stitches, then turn the work over *from left to right*, and make 1 chain stitch.

Row 2 Single crochet over these 8 stitches for 1 row.

Row 3 Make a decrease by single crocheting 2 stitches together (see page 65) at the beginning and end of the row, so that you have a total of 6 stitches.

You need never make the
same hat twice when you
know how to create so many
simple variations.

Continue to work, decreasing on every *other* row, until you have a total of 2 stitches. To finish, make a final decrease by single crocheting the last 2 stitches together so that you have 1 stitch remaining, and end off. If you want your earflaps to have ties, make 20 to 25 chain stitches, depending on how long you want them, then end off.

To make the second earflap, attach a new strand of yarn to the last round of the hat, 12 stitches to the left of the first earflap. Then repeat the steps for making the first earflap. If desired, make tassels and attach them to the ends of the earflaps or ties (see right).

to make a hat with a pointy top

Follow directions on page 82 for getting the first round of a circle started, but only make 4 single crochet stitches into the second chain stitch, rather than the usual 6. *Place a marker in the last stitch of the round, and remember to move it to the last stitch of each round throughout the remainder of the pattern.*

Round 2 Single crochet around without making any increases, so that you still have 4 stitches at the end of the round.

Round 3 Increase by making 2 single crochet stitches in every stitch, which will bring you to the end of the round, and you will have a total of 8 stitches.

Round 4 *Single crochet in the next stitch, then make an increase in the 2nd stitch.* Repeat the instructions between the asterisks 3 more times, which will bring you to the end of the round, and you will have a total of 12 stitches.

Round 5 *Single crochet in the next 2 stitches, and then make an increase in the 3rd stitch.* Repeat the instruction between the asterisks 3 more times, which will bring you to the end of the round, and you will have a total of 18 stitches.

Continue to work, increasing on every round, adding 1 to the number of single crochet stitches you make before increasing. Do this for 4 more rows, until you have a total of 42 single crochet stitches. Then proceed with steps above for making the body of the hat. If desired, make tassels and attach them to the ends of the earflaps or ties (see right).

Making Tassels

Tassels are a simple way to decorate your crocheted hats. Of course, they can also be attached to other items, including scarves and the corners of blankets and pillows.

1 Cut a rectangle out of cardboard, about 2 inches wide and about 4 to 5 inches long, depending on how long you want your tassels to be. Wrap a strand of yarn around the cardboard, lengthwise, about 8 to 10 times. Then, pass an 8- to 10-inch strand of yarn under the top end of the wrapped bundle on the cardboard, and tie it in a double knot. Cut the wrapped bundle at the bottom end of the cardboard with scissors.

2 Pull down one of the ends coming from the double knot and wrap it around the center of bundle near the top a couple of times, then stitch it down through the bundle. Trim any uneven ends with scissors. Use the other end at the top of the tassel to attach it to the end of the earflaps or chains on your hat.

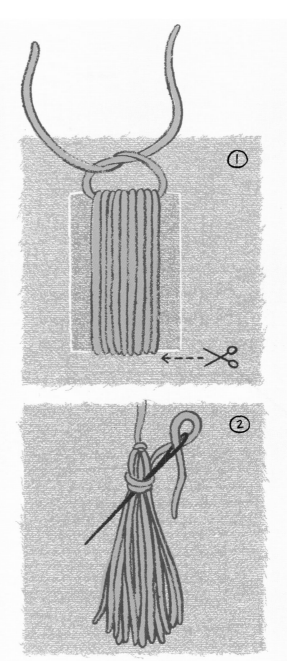

small stuffed
shapes

Now it's time to take all of the skills
you've learned and combine them to create
three-dimensional objects like the Juggling Balls (page 100),
Cupcake Pincushion (page 104), and Doll Friends (page 108)
in this chapter. You've already learned how gradually
increasing stitches as you crochet in the round keeps your
circle flat, and how crocheting in the round without
increasing stitches creates a tubular shape. Now it's time to
decrease stitches in the round, which will allow you to close up a
tubular shape after stuffing it with a filler, such as beans.
The trick is to make sure your stitches are small and tight,
so that the filler won't stick out or fall through the spaces
between the stitches. To achieve this you will work with a hook
quite a bit smaller than any of the hooks you have
worked with up to this point.

juggling balls

Each of these balls is made in one continuous piece of circular crochet. Make a few and fill them with beans, so they'll be good for juggling. Or make just one and use it as a kick sack. Practice making one in a single color at first. Then try making some with rings of color by switching colors at the end of a round (see page 85). You can use some of the beans to help you keep track of what round you are on when you are making the body of the sack: Start with a pile of 10 beans, then take one away with each round.

materials *(for one ball)*

APPROXIMATELY 25 YARDS SPORTWEIGHT MERCERIZED COTTON YARN, SUCH AS TAHKI COTTON CLASSIC

SIZE F (3.75 MM) CROCHET HOOK

SPLIT-RING STITCH MARKER OR SAFETY PIN

ABOUT $1/3$ CUP LIGHT-COLORED, MEDIUM-SIZE DRIED BEANS, SUCH AS SOYBEANS

YARN NEEDLE

gauge

THE FIRST 2 ROUNDS OF THE PATTERN = $1 \, 1/2$ INCHES

A single ball makes a great kick sack!

make top of ball

Follow directions on page 82 for getting the first round of a circle started. Make sure you have 6 single crochet stitches at the end of the round. *Do not use a marker at this point.*

Round 2 *Make an increase in the first stitch by making 2 single crochet stitches in the same stitch (see page 64).* Repeat the instruction between the asterisks 21 more times, until you have a total of 28 stitches. Place a marker in the last stitch. *Remember, at the end of each new round, count the total number of stitches, and then move the marker to the last stitch.*

make body of ball

Single crochet around without making any increases for 10 rounds. *To help keep track of what round you are on, write down the numbers 1 through 10 on a piece of paper, and check off the number for each round as you complete it.* At the end of the last round, remove the marker.

make bottom of ball

Round 12 *Single crochet in the next 3 stitches, then make a decrease by single crocheting 2 stitches together (see page 65).* Repeat the instruction between the asterisks 6 more times, until you have a total of 21 stitches. Fill the ball halfway with beans.

Round 13 *Single crochet in the next 2 stitches, then make a decrease.* Repeat the instruction between the asterisks 6 more times, until you have a total of 14 stitches.

Round 14 *Single crochet in the next stitch, then make a decrease.* Repeat the instruction between the asterisks 8 more times, until you have a total of 5 stitches.

End off (see page 84), leaving about a 6-inch long tail. Push more beans through the opening, until the ball is firm. Thread the tail with a yarn needle, and stitch through the remaining stitches as shown below. Pull the tail to draw the stitches together and make a knot. Push the yarn needle through the ball to the other side, then cut the tail.

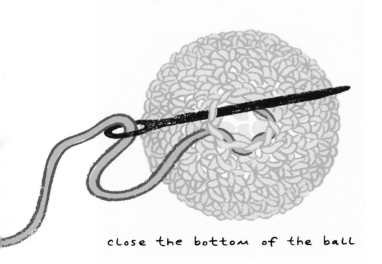

close the bottom of the ball

Mastering Tight Stitches

When you are making stuffed shapes, it's important to keep the stitches tight so that the stuffing doesn't poke out.

If you have trouble keeping your stitches tight, try wrapping the working yarn twice around your index finger. To do this, follow step 1 of the instructions on page 20 for how to hold the yarn, then loop your index finger through the yarn once more before turning your palm to face you, and proceed with the remaining steps.

cupcake pincushion

This frosty cupcake pincushion makes a great birthday gift for a friend who likes to do needlework (or just likes cupcakes). Make the bottom and the icing top in two separate pieces and then sew them together. Weight the bottom down by filling it with beans, so it won't tip over easily, and fill the top with stuffing, to create a cushion for straight pins. The icing top on the cupcake in the photograph was made with fuzzy "vanilla" angora yarn, but you can make yours any "flavor" you like. A dash of seed beads makes great pretend sprinkles.

materials

APPROXIMATELY 15 YARDS SPORTWEIGHT YARN FOR THE BOTTOM, AND 15 YARDS WORSTED-WEIGHT YARN FOR THE TOP. (SHOWN IN CLASSIC ELITE WATERSPUN FELTED MERINO FOR THE BOTTOM AND CLASSIC ELITE LUSH FOR THE TOP)

SIZE F (3.75 MM) CROCHET HOOK

SPLIT-RING MARKER OR SAFETY PIN

YARN NEEDLE

APPROXIMATELY 20 SEED BEADS (AVAILABLE AT GENERAL CRAFT AND BEAD STORES)

SMALL SEWING NEEDLE THIN ENOUGH TO PASS THROUGH HOLES IN SEED BEADS

SEWING THREAD

ABOUT $^1/_3$ CUP LIGHT-COLORED, MEDIUM-SIZE DRIED BEANS, SUCH AS SOYBEANS

HANDFUL OF COTTON OR SYNTHETIC FIBER STUFFING

gauge

THE FIRST 3 ROUNDS OF THE PATTERN = $1 \frac{1}{2}$ INCHES

make cupcake bottom

Follow steps 1 through 6 of instructions on pages 82–83 for getting the first 3 rounds of a circle started. Make sure you have a total of 18 stitches at the end of the third round. Then check to make sure your gauge is correct for this pattern (page 88), and move the marker to the last stitch. *Remember, at the end of each new round, count the total number of stitches, then move the marker to the last stitch.* This project will work if you don't match your gauge exactly but you should make sure that your crocheted fabric isn't too loose; if it is, the stuffing may stick out between the stitches. Basically, the tighter the stitches are together (the more stitches there are per inch) the better.

Round 4 *Single crochet in the next 2 stitches, then make an increase by making 2 single crochet stitches in the 3rd stitch (page 64).* Repeat the instruction between the asterisks 5 more times. This will bring you to the end of the round, and you will have a total of 24 stitches.

Round 5 Begin working in the BACK LOOPS ONLY of each stitch (see page 52). *Single crochet in the next 2 stitches, then make a decrease by single crocheting 2 stitches together (see page 65).* Repeat the instruction between the asterisks 5 more times. This will bring you to the end of the round, and you will have a total of 18 stitches.

Round 6 Resume working in BOTH LOOPS of each stitch for the remainder of the pattern. Repeat round 4. You will have a total of 24 stitches.

Round 7 *Single crochet in the next 3 stitches, then make an increase in the 4th stitch.* Repeat the instruction in between the asterisks 5 more times. This will bring you to the end of the round, and you will have a total of 30 stitches.

Round 8 Single crochet for 4 rounds without making any increases. *To help keep track of what round you are on, write down the numbers 1 through 4 on a piece of paper, and check off the number for each round as you complete it.* End off, leaving about a 10-inch tail.

make icing top

1 Repeat instructions for making the bottom, up to round 4, then single crochet for 4 rounds without making any increases.

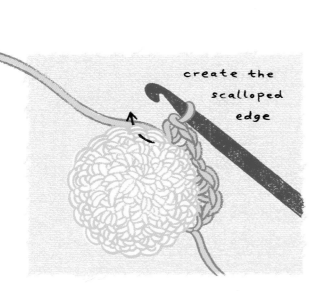

create the
scalloped
edge

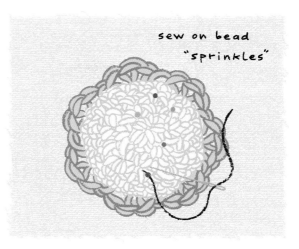

sew on bead
"sprinkles"

2 To create the scalloped edge: *Make 3 single crochet stitches in the next stitch. Then skip over the second stitch and make a slipstitch in the 3rd stitch. * Repeat the instruction between the asterisks 9 more times. End off and weave the tail in on the wrong side.

assemble and decorate cupcake

1 Place the icing top piece over the bottom piece, lining up the stitches on the top edge of the bottom with the inside of the scalloped edge of the top. Then thread the tail from the bottom piece with a yarn needle and stitch the 2 pieces together with the woven stitch (see page 43). Stop stitching halfway around and fill up the bottom with beans. Then fill the top with some stuffing, and continue stitching the 2 pieces together. When you are done, knot and push the needle through the cupcake to the other side. Cut the remaining tail.

2 Decorate your cupcake with a sprinkling of seed beads. Get your thread and needle started as you would for sewing on a button (see page 31). *Remember that you will need to work with a sewing needle that is thin enough to pass through the hole in your beads.* One at a time, sew on each bead as follows: Pass the bead over the tip of the needle, and bring it down to where the thread is attached to the cupcake. Then hold the bead in place with your index finger and put your needle into the cupcake right next to the bead and bring the needle back up at the point where you want the next bead to be. When you are done attaching all of the beads, knot the thread and push the needle through the cupcake to the other side. Cut the remaining thread.

doll friends

These cute dolls are all made from the same pattern. The head and the body are made in one piece. The arms, legs, and bear's ears and snout, are made separately and sewn on afterwards. You can make a whole cast of characters by simply altering the color of yarn that you use to make the body or the hair. Tiny buttons for eyes, and a couple of red stitches or a bead for a mouth, give each doll its own unique personality.

doll

make doll's head

Follow steps 1 through 6 of instructions on pages 82–83 for getting the first three rounds of a circle started. Make sure you have a total of 18 stitches at the end of the third round. Then check to make sure your gauge is correct for this pattern (page 88). *Remember, at the end of each round, count the total*

materials

SPORTWEIGHT YARN: TO MAKE THE DOLL OR THE BEAR, YOU WILL NEED APPROXIMATELY 105 YARDS. FOR THE DOLL'S DRESS, YOU WILL NEED APPROXIMATELY 30 YARDS, FOR THE DOLL'S HAIR, ABOUT 10 YARDS, AND FOR THE BEAR'S SCARF ABOUT 6 YARDS. (FOR SPECIFIC INFORMATION ABOUT YARNS USED FOR DOLLS SHOWN, SEE PAGE 126.)

SIZE F (3.75 MM) HOOK

SPLIT-RING MARKER OR SAFETY PIN

YARN NEEDLE

A FEW HANDFULS OF COTTON OR SYNTHETIC FIBER STUFFING

SMALL BUTTONS FOR EYES AND/OR MOUTH

REGULAR SEWING THREAD AND A SEWING NEEDLE THAT WILL FIT THROUGH THE HOLES ON THE BUTTONS

A BIT OF RED YARN OR EMBROIDERY THREAD FOR THE DOLL'S MOUTH

gauge

THE FIRST 3 ROUNDS OF THE PATTERN = $1\frac{1}{2}$ INCHES

number of stitches, *then move the marker to the last stitch.* This project will work if you don't match your gauge exactly but you should make sure that your crocheted fabric isn't too loose; if it is, the stuffing may stick out between the stitches. Basically, the tighter the stitches are together (the more stitches there are per inch) the better.

Round 4 *Single crochet in the next 2 stitches, then make an increase by making 2 single crochet stitches in the 3rd stitch (see page 64).* Repeat the instruction between the asterisks a total of 6 times until you reach the marker. Then continue past the marker, repeating the instruction between the asterisks another 2 times until you have a total of 26 stitches. Move the marker to the last stitch.

Single crochet around without making any increases for 6 rounds. *To help keep track of what round you are on, write down the numbers 1 through 6 on a piece of paper, and check off the number for each round as you complete it.*

Round 11 *Single crochet in the next 3 stitches, then make a decrease by single crocheting 2 stitches together (see page 65).* Repeat the instruction between the asterisks 4 more times, until you are one stitch in front of the marker. Then continue past the marker, repeating the instructions between the asterisks 2 more times, until you have a total of 19 stitches. Move the marker to the last stitch.

Round 12 *Single crochet in the next 2 stitches, then make a decrease by single crocheting 2 stitches together. *Repeat the instruction between the asterisks 4 more times, going past the marker by 1 stitch, until you have a total of 14 stitches. Move the marker to the last stitch.

Round 13 *Single crochet in the next stitch, then make a decrease by single crocheting 2 stitches together.* Repeat the instruction between the asterisks 3 more times, ending 1 stitch before the marker, at which point you will have a total of 10 stitches. Move the marker to the last stitch.

Single crochet around without making any decreases for 2 rounds, then fill the head with some stuffing before continuing.

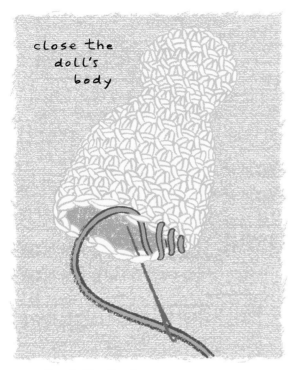

close the doll's body

make doll's body

Round 16 *Single crochet in the next stitch, then make an increase in the 2nd stitch.* Repeat the instruction between the asterisks another 7 times, until you have a total of 18 stitches. Move the marker to the last stitch.

Round 17 Single crochet in the next 2 stitches, then make an increase by making 2 single crochet stitches in the 3rd stitch. Repeat the instruction between the aster-

isks another 7 times, until you have a total of 26 stitches. Move the marker again.

Then single crochet around without making any increases for 15 more rounds, and end off (page 84), leaving about a 6-inch-long tail.

To finish, fill the neck and body with more stuffing. Then thread the tail with a yarn needle, flatten the opening, and sew it shut with the woven stitch (see page 43).

make doll's arms

Follow directions on page 82 for getting the first round of a circle started.

Round 2 *Single crochet in the next stitch, then make an increase in the 2nd stitch.* Repeat the instruction between the asterisks 2 more times, until you have a total of 9 stitches.

Then single crochet around without making any increases for 16 rounds, and end off, leaving a 6-inch-long tail. Repeat to make a second arm. Fill the arms with stuffing and stitch the openings shut the same way you did for the body.

make doll's legs

Follow directions on page 82 for getting the first 2 rounds of a circle started. Then single crochet around without making any increases for 16 rounds, and end off. Repeat to make a second leg. Fill the legs with stuffing and stitch the openings shut the same way you did for the body.

assemble doll

Sew the arms to either side of the body, a little less than an inch from the neck, and sew the legs to the bottom seam of the body.

make doll's face

Use the same yarn you used to make the doll's body for the nose, and a bit of red yarn or embroidery thread for the mouth. For both, get the yarn started in the back of the head with a couple of stitches, then push the needle to the front. For the nose, bring the needle up in the center of the doll's head, and tie the strand of yarn in a few knots. When the nose is the size you want it to be, push the needle down next to the knots, pulling the remaining yarn through to the back of the head, and weave the tail in. For the mouth, bring the needle to the front, about $\frac{1}{4}$ inch under the nose,

and make a couple of tiny stitches, then pull the remaining yarn through to the back of the head, and weave in the tail. Sew on tiny buttons for eyes (see page 31 if you don't know how to sew on a button).

make doll's hair

For long hair, cut about 25 (10-inch) strands of worsted-weight yarn, and for short hair, cut about 25 (7-inch) strands. To attach a length of hair, thread one of the strands onto a yarn needle, then pass the needle through a center stitch on the top of the head. Pull the yarn through so that you have an even amount of yarn on either side of the stitch, then tie the strand in a knot. Repeat with the rest of the hair. For ponytails, group the strands on either side of the head, then stitch them in place with a contrasting color of yarn.

make dress

Work in rows. To make the front of the dress, begin with a foundation row of 15 chain stitches.

Row 1 Follow directions on page 24 for single crochet, and single crochet for 1 row. *Remember to count your stitches at the end of the row. If you began with 15 chain stitches, you should now have 14 stitches in the row. Always turn the work from right to left at the end of each row, and make one chain stitch before beginning the next row.*

Row 2 Make a decrease, by single crocheting 2 stitches together, once at the beginning and once at the end of the row. You will have a total of 12 stitches.

Then single crochet for 5 rows.

Row 8 Make an increase at the beginning and at the end of the row, so you have a total of 14 stitches.

Continue to work, increasing on every 5th row, until you have a total of 20 stitches.

Then single crochet for 5 rows, and end off, leaving about a 10-inch tail.

Repeat to make the back of the dress.

assemble dress

Block the front and back pieces (see page 34), and place them with the wrong sides together. Using the woven stitch (see page 43), create the shoulder seams at the top of the dress by sewing the last 2 stitches at either ends of the foundation rows of both pieces together. Then sew the side seams together, leaving about a $1^1/_4$-inch opening at the top ends for the armholes. Weave in the tails on the wrong sides (the inside) of the dress. To put the dress on the doll, slip it over the feet first, rather than the head.

bear

Follow the directions for making the doll's head, body, arms, and legs.

make bear's ears, snout, and scarf

To make the ears, make one round of 6 single crochet stitches, and end off. Repeat to make a second ear. Stitch the ears to the top of the bear's head with the woven stitch. To make the snout, work 2 rounds of circular crochet, so that you have 12 single crochet stitches in the 2nd round, and then end off. Fill the tiny snout with a bit of stuffing and then stitch it to the front of the bear's face with the leftover tail.

To make the scarf, begin with a foundation row of 4 chain stitches, and single crochet for about 50 rows, or until it is about 11 inches long.

Crochet Around the World

NO ONE KNOWS EXACTLY WHERE OR WHEN PEOPLE FIRST BEGAN CROCHETING,
BUT EXAMPLES OF CROCHET CAN BE FOUND IN MANY AREAS OF THE WORLD.

In **Scandinavia**, a simple form of crochet called *pjoning*, or *patning* was used to create warm garments in the 1800s. This technique, also known as *sheperd's knitting*, is a slip-stitch done through the front or back loop of each stitch, and was often done in intricate, colorful patterns.

Ireland is known for *Irish Crochet*—a form of crocheted lace made up of motifs (such as shamrocks and flowers)—used to make copies of more expensive "true" lace articles such as collars, parasols, gloves, even entire dresses. The income from these articles helped the Irish to survive the famine of the 1800s. At the beginning of the 20th century, Irish crochet also became an economic staple in Brittany, **France**, where the traditional costume for women consists of many lace pieces, including a headdress known as a *coiffe* (pronounced *kwahff*).

The pioneer girls and women of **North America** were known for crocheting items out of leftover scraps of yarn or rags. The *granny square* is a well-known development of this kind of "scrap crochet," and is still popular today. The squares are crocheted individually and then sewn together to create larger items, such as blankets and shawls.

A form of crochet known as *tapestry crochet* looks and feels like weaving but is used to create hats in many parts of the world. The *kufi cap*, or the *kajaya* (pronounced *koo faa*), is a traditional prayer cap worn by men in Morocco. In West Cameroon, **Africa** special hats are crocheted and worn to commemorate important events. In **Jamaica**, and other parts of the **Carribean**, men and women wear large, round crocheted caps known as a *tams* to keep their dreadlocks in place. The small, round cap worn by Jewish men —called a *yarmulke* (pronounced *ya-ma-ka*) or a *kippa*—is also typically crocheted. In **Guatemala**, a tapestry-crocheted bag is an important part of a Mayan Indian man's traditional outfit.

your *first* sweater

You have now learned everything you need to
know to make your first sweater, and you're more than ready!
The Rib Stitch Pullover is super-easy to make.
There are no new stitches to learn, and no fancy
finishing techniques. The body is made of two large
rectangles, the sleeves are two triangular pieces,
and the hood, which is optional, is one long rectangle
folded in half. What could be more simple? The only
trick is that it will take a while to complete,
so relax, and work on it when you have a lot of free
time—for instance, on rainy days or on long car trips.
Keep your project all together in one bag so that
you always know where it is, and remember to keep good notes
about what row you are on whenever you stop working.
If you don't, you may be confused about where you are in
the pattern when you start working again.

rib stitch
pullover

This pullover is made with the front-loop version of the rib stitch (see page 52). This stitch is perfect for crocheting sweaters, because it requires less yarn than the single crochet stitch, and because it creates a more flexible fabric that hangs nicely. Chelsea, Sofia, and Sadie-Mae, along with Lola on page 117, are all wearing variations of this same sweater. Sadie-Mae, Sofia, and Lola's pullovers were made with one strand of bulky yarn, but Chelsea's blue and brown heathered pullover was made with a blue strand of bulky yarn combined with a worsted-weight strand of brown yarn, and that's why hers is a little bigger.

figure out your size

To help figure out your size for this project, pick a favorite sweatshirt or sweater to use as a guide. Lay it down on a flat surface and measure across from underarm to underarm. This will give you the measurement for the width of the front and back pieces of your sweater. For example, if your sweatshirt measures about 14 inches across, you should follow instructions for size 8 when making your pullover. If the

materials

Solid-color pullover: APPROXIMATELY 650 (640, 785, 830) YARDS BULKY YARN

Heathered pullover: 665 (730, 815, 870) YARDS *EACH* BULKY AND WORSTED-WEIGHT YARN (FOR SPECIFIC INFORMATION ABOUT YARNS USED FOR PULLOVERS SHOWN, SEE PAGE 126)

SIZE M (9.00MM) CROCHET HOOK

YARN NEEDLE

ABOUT 6 SPLIT-RING STITCH MARKERS OR SAFETY PINS

sizes

8 (10, 12, 14) YEARS

finished measurements
Plain: 30 (32, 34, 36)"
Heathered: 38 (40, 43, 45)"

gauge

Plain: 10 SINGLE CROCHET STITCHES AND 8 ROWS= 4" IN SINGLE CROCHET THROUGH FRONT LOOP

Heathered: 8 STITCHES AND 7 ROWS = 4" IN SINGLE CROCHET THROUGH FRONT LOOP

measurement you get falls between sizes, round up or round down to the next size. *Keep in mind that if you base your size on an oversized sweatshirt, your pullover will also end up being nice and roomy, but if you choose a more close-fitting sweater, your pullover will end up being more snug.*

make a gauge swatch

To get started, make a swatch to test your gauge. Start with a foundation row of 12 chain stitches, and work in single crochet for 9 rows. Then, without stretching or squishing, pin the swatch down to a flat surface, such as a towel, and measure the number of single crochet stitches you have over 4 inches. If you are making a pullover with a single strand of yarn, you want 10 single crochet stitches and 8 rows to be equal to 4 inches. If the number of stitches that is equal to 4 inches is less than 10, then make another swatch with a smaller hook, and if it is more, then make one with a larger hook. If you are making a heathered pullover by crocheting with 2 different-colored strands of yarn at the same time, you want 8 single crochet stitches and 7 rows to be equal to 4 inches. If the number of stitches that is equal to 4 inches is less than 8, then make another swatch with a smaller hook, and if it is more, then make one with a larger hook. *Keep in mind*

that working with a double strand of yarn will cause the overall size of your finished pullover to be larger than one made with a single strand of yarn. Keep on making test swatches until you achieve the correct gauge.

circle your size

This pattern is written for a solid-color pullover in 4 sizes. Circle in pencil the numbers that correspond to your size, for each row in the instructions.

make pullover front and back

NOTE: Work the Heathered pullover the same as the Solid pullover except where noted.

Begin with a foundation row of 39 (41, 44, 46) chain stitches (page 22).

Follow directions for single crochet on page 24, and single crochet for 1 row. Remember to count your stitches at the end of the row. If you began with 39 (41, 44, 46) chain stitches, you should now have 38 (40, 43, 45) stitches in the row. Always turn your work from right to left at the end each of row, and make 1 chain stitch before beginning the next row. If you are making a striped pullover, switch colors at the end of a row (see page 38 for directions on attaching a new color).

On the 2nd row, begin the rib stitch (see page 52), working in the FRONT LOOPS ONLY of each stitch. Continue until the rectangle measures 18 (19, 20, 21) inches from top to bottom. End off and weave in tails. Repeat to make the back.

make sleeves

Begin with a foundation row of 22 (22, 24, 24) chain stitches.

Single crochet for 1 row. You should have 21 (21, 23, 23) single crochet stitches in the row.

On the second row, begin working in rib stitch (see page 52), making single crochet stitches in the FRONT LOOPS ONLY of each stitch to the end of the row.

Continue to work in rib stitch for 2 more rows. On the 5th row, make an increase (page 64), by making 2 rib stitches in the front loop of the same stitch, once at the beginning of the row, and once at the end of the row. This will add 2 stitches to the row, so you should have 23 (23, 25, 25) stitches at the end of the row.

If you are making the heathered pullover, skip forward to instructions below at this point.

Continue working in rib stitch, without making any increases for 2 rows.

On the 3rd row, increase at the beginning and end of the row so that you have a total of 25 (25, 27, 27) stitches.

Continue to work, increasing at the beginning and end of every 3rd row another 5 (6, 7, 8) times, until you have a total of 35 (37, 41, 43) stitches. To help keep track of what row you are on, place a stitch marker in the last stitch of each row that you increase on.

Finally, continue working in rib stitch without making any increases, until the piece measures 15.5 (16, 16.5, 17) inches from top to bottom. End off, leaving a 24-inch tail. Repeat for the second sleeve.

For the Heathered Pullover:
Follow directions above for making sleeves up to the 5th row.

Continue working in rib stitch without making any increases for 3 rows, and then increase at the beginning and end of the 4th row.

Continue to work, increasing at the beginning and end of every 4th row another 2 (3, 3, 4) times, until you have a total of 29 (31, 33, 35) stitches.

Finally, continue working in rib stitch without making any increases until the piece measures

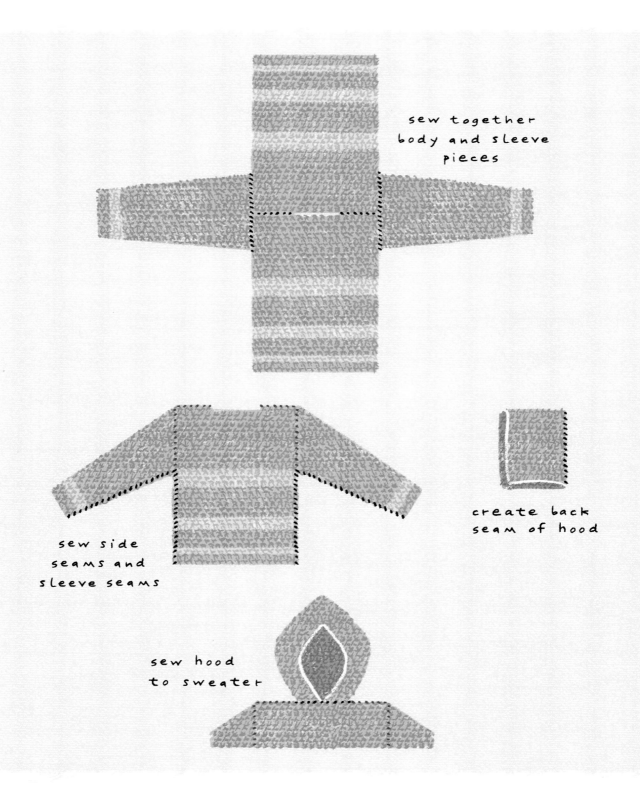

sew together
body and sleeve
pieces

create back
seam of hood

sew side
seams and
sleeve seams

sew hood
to sweater

13.5 (14, 14.25, 14.75) inches from top to bottom. End off, leaving a 24-inch tail. Repeat for the second sleeve.

make hood (optional)

Begin with a long foundation row of 61 (61, 61, 61) chain stitches, and working in the FRONT LOOPS ONLY, single crochet for 19 (19, 20, 20) rows (60 single crochet stitches in each row). End off, leaving about an 18-inch tail.

For the Heathered Pullover:

Begin with a long foundation row of 49 (49, 49, 49) chain stitches, and working in the FRONT LOOPS ONLY, single crochet for 17 (17, 18, 18) rows (48 single crochet stitches in each row). End off, leaving about an 18-inch tail.

assemble pullover

Begin by blocking each of the pieces so they lay nice and flat (see page 34). Then lay the front and back pieces out, with the right sides facing up (page 27), on a large, flat, clean surface.

To create the shoulder seams: Line up the edges of the last rows on both pieces so they're touching (see illustration at left). Using stitch markers or safety pins, mark off a 9.5

(9.5, 10, 10) -inch section in the middle for the neck opening. Then using the woven stitch (page 43), sew the shoulder seams from the markers to the outside edges.

To attach the sleeves: Place markers or safety pins 7 (7.5, 8, 8.5) inches down from each shoulder seam on the front and back pieces. Then using the woven stitch, sew the sleeves in between the markers, matching the center stitch of the sleeve with the shoulder seam.

Fold the entire piece in half, with the wrong sides facing each other, and sew the side and underarm seams with the woven stitch.

To attach the hood: Fold the hood piece in half, lengthwise, with the wrong sides facing each other. Create the back seam of the hood by sewing the sides together along one of the long edges with the woven stitch. Then pin the two front corners to the center of the neck opening in the front, and the back seam to the center of neck opening in the back. Attach the hood to the neck opening with the woven stitch. Weave in leftover yarn tails on the wrong side of the work.

Caring for Your Crochet

Keep your crocheted projects in good shape by washing and storing carefully.

washing

Items crocheted with synthetic yarns, such as acrylic, can usually be machine washed, but items crocheted with natural yarns, such as wool, generally need to be hand-washed. Care information is usually indicated on yarn labels. If unsure, handwash the item. Always wash with a mild detergent, or with a cleaning product specially formulated for washing wool garments. Eucalan and Wool Mix (available at most yarn shops) are great products because you don't need to rinse them out. Follow the instructions on the detergent label or those that follow.

1 Fill a sink or bathtub with lukewarm water. Add a capful of detergent, or amount recommended on label. Place the item in the water and gently move around (no scrubbing or twisting). Let soak in the water for about 10 minutes.

2 If using a no-rinse detergent, skip to step 3. If using regular detergent, gently squeeze the soapy water from the item as tub drains. Remove the item, then refill tub with fresh, lukewarm water. Place item back in the water and gently squeeze. Repeat this process until there are no soapsuds left.

3 Lift item from tub, supporting its weight with your hands so it doesn't stretch and lay it flat on a thick, dry towel. Roll up the towel and the item together, then gently press down so the towel absorbs the water, then unroll.

4 Lay the item flat on another dry towel on a water-resistant surface that is not too close to direct heat sources, such as a radiator, and where it is safe from pets and out of direct sunlight. Arrange into its original shape and leave to dry.

storing

Always store crocheted items on a shelf or in a drawer. Do not place on hangers as this will cause stretching. To keep moths away, keep crocheted items clean (moths like food stains and body oils) and store them with a natural repellent like cedar chips or a small sachet of dried herbs, such as lavender or rosemary.

Reading Crochet Patterns

Up to this point, all of the crochet patterns in this book have been written for beginners, with detailed, step-by-step instructions. As you move on to exploring more advanced patterns in other books, you will notice that often the patterns are written with abbreviations. Luckily, most of these abbreviations are standardized so that once you learn what they stand for, you will be able to understand just about any pattern you come across. The following is a list of some of the most common abbreviations. Some of the abbreviations are for stitches that aren't taught in this book, such as double and triple crochet. Illustrated instructions for most of these stitches can be found in more advanced crochet books.

common abbreviations

approx	approximately
beg	begin(ning)
BLO	back loop only
FLO	front loop only
CC	contrasting color
ch	chain
cm	centimeters
cont	continue/ing
dc	double crochet
dec	decrease/decreasing
g or gr	grams
hdc	half double crochet
inc	increase/increasing
"	inch(es)
lp(s)	loop(s)
MC	main color
mm	millimeters
oz	ounces
patt(s)	pattern(s)
rem	remaining
rep	repeat
rnd(s)	round(s) (rows worked in a circle)
RS	right side
sc	single crochet
sl st	slip stitch
sp(s)	space(s)
st(s)	stitch(es)
tog	together
tr	triple
WS	wrong side
yd(s)	yard(s)
yo	yarn over hook

Yarn Resources

Following is a list of all of the yarns used for the projects shown in **Kids Crochet**.

Neck Cozy
Page 29: Cascade Magnum in rust (#9463)

Tool Pouch (page 33)
Wooly Hill Farm Worsted in lavender and light blue

Friendship Cuffs (page 41)
Cascade 220 in light blue (#7815) and persimmon (#4146); Brown Sheep Nature Spun Worsted in bougainvillea (#105), bit of blue (#115), orange you glad (#N54), and spring green (#09)
Brown Sheep Lamb's Pride Superwash Worsted in Les Brown (#SW37)

Striped Bags (page 45)
3-color version: Brown Sheep Lamb's Pride Bulky in crème (#M10), lotus pink (#M38), and orange you glad (#M110)
Multicolored version: Classic Elite Lush in brown (#4438) and Wooly Hill Farm Worsted in pink, brown, light blue, and cream combined with Koigu Premium Merino Worsted in brown (#2399)

Ribbed Scarves
(Page 51) Tahki Dazzle in pink/brown/orange (#003)
Page 55: Cascade 220 in cordovan (#9408), baby heather rose (#9442), persimmon (#4146), and beige (#8021) for pink and brown scarf; summer sky heather (#9452), celery (#9407), and Lake Chelan heather (#9451) for blue and green version

Patchwork Poncho (page 59)
Brown Sheep Nature Spun and Lamb's Pride Superwash Worsted (see *Friendship Cuffs* above for colors); Cascade 220 (see Ribbed

Scarves above for colors); Koigu Premium Merino Worsted in brown (#2399), light green (#2351), light blue (#2151), and orange (#1220); Tahki New Tweed in lavender (#019), blue (#017), green (#015), and brown/white (#025); and Tahki Jolie in light blue (#5015)

Headband (page 67)
Tahki New Tweed in lavender (# 019)

Triangle-Square Quilt (page 72)
Brown Sheep Nature Spun Worsted in bougainvillea (#105) and bit of blue (#115) and Brown Sheep Lamb's Pride Superwash worsted in Les Brown (#SW37)

Triangle-Square Pillow (page 71)
Brown Sheep Nature Spun Worsted in orange you glad (#N54) and Brown Sheep Lamb's Pride Superwash Worsted in alabaster (#SW10) and blaze (#SW145)

Critter Cushions (page 87)
Crystal Palace Iceland Bulky in glacier blue (#2013), pumpkin (#0022), fuchsia (#1219), and oat (#6885)

Hat Trick (page 92)
Page 93: Blue with buttons: Morehouse Farm Bulky in light blue
Page 95: All hats were made with Brown Sheep Lamb's Pride Bulky except where noted: sandy heather (#M01) and rust (#M97) combined with Koigu Premium Merino worsted in orange (#1220) and Tahki Jolie in light blue (#5015) for gray/orange/blue version; almond blossom (#M86) for beige version; crème (#M10) combined with Koigu premium merino worsted in red (#2227) for white/red version; blue magic (#M77), misty blue (#M76), and limeade (# M120) for blue/green version; Reynolds Lopi Bulky in light denim heather (#8), crimson (#434), and white (#51) for blue/red/white version

Juggling Balls (page 101)
Tahki Cotton Classic in green (#3713), blue (#3837), yellow (#3525), and red (#3411)

Cupcake Pincushion (page 105)
Cupcake bottom in Classic Elite Waterspun in blue (#5029) and cupcake top in Classic Elite Lush in white (#4416)

Doll Friends (page 109)
Brunette: Tahki Cotton Classic in beige (#3220) for body, Classic Elite Bazic in Grizzley (#2976) for hair, and Koigu premium merino in pink (#1100) and fuchsia (#2233) for dress
Redhead: Tahki Cotton Classic in peach (#3472) for body, Classic Elite Inca Alpaca in Harvest Bounty (#1155) for hair, and Koigu premium merino in blue (#1005) and lavender (#1013) for dress
Bear: Rowan Kid Classic in Bear (#817) for body and Classic Elite Inca Alpaca in cala cala moss (#1135) for scarf

Rib Stitch Pullover
Page 119: Brown Sheep Lamb's Pride Bulky in oregano (#M113) for dark green version, Reynolds Lopi Bulky in Light Denim Heather (#8), Crimson (#434) and white (#51) for blue with red and white stripe version
Page 119: Brown Sheep Lamb's Pride Bulky in wild oak (#M08) with stripes in Morehouse Farm bulky in fuchsia, soft pink, and chocolate brown
Page 117: Reynolds Lopi Bulky in light Berry heather (#2)
Page 119: Morehouse Farm Bulky in light blue and pumpkin for orange and blue version; Morehouse Farm Bulky in light blue and Morehouse Farm worsted in chocolate brown for the heathered version. Reynolds Lopi Bulky in mulberry (#84) and smokey fuschia (#209) for the pink version.

If you can't find the yarns listed here in your local yarn shop, try contacting the companies that make and distribute them directly.

Morehouse Farm
141 Milan Hill Road, Milan, NY 12571
866-470-4852, www.morehousefarm.com

Tahki • Stacy Charles
70-30 80th St., Bldg 36, Ridgewood, NY 11385
800-338-YARN, www.tahkistacycharles.com

Koigu Yarns
RR # 1, Williamsford, Ontario
NoH 2Vo CANADA
888-765-WOOL, www.koigu.com

Brown Sheep Yarn Company
100662 Country Road 16, Mitchell, NE 69357
800-826-9136, www.brownsheep.com

Cascade Yarns
1224 Andover Park East, Tukila, WA 98138
206-574-0440, www.cascadeyarns.com

Reynolds Yarns
35 Scales Lane, Townsend, MA 01469-1094
978-597-8794, www.jcacrafts.com

Classic Elite Yarns
300 Jackson Street, Lowell, MA 01852
978-453-2837, www.classiceliteyarns.com

Wooly Hill Farm
207 Mumford Road, Jordanville, NY 13361
315-868-1568

Rowan Yarns/Westminster Fibers
4 Townsend West, Unit 8, Nashnar, NH 03063
800-445-9276, www.knitrowan.com

Magic Cabin Dolls (for 100% wool felt)
888-623-3655, www.magiccabin.com

Clothing Provided by:
Flora and Henri
888-749-9698; www.florahenri.com

Estella
212-255-3553; www.estella-nyc.com.

Acknowledgments

Making a book like *Kids Crochet* takes a lot of teamwork. I was lucky to have the following talented and committed players on my team: Lena Corwin created all of the illustrations with a unique style that far surpassed my dreams, and Jennifer Wagner designed each page with ingenious whimsy. John Gruen got up on a ladder and stood out in the cold for hours to get the very best photographs. My mother stopped everything in her life to crochet all the triangles for the pillow and quilt projects, and Steffi Lynen, Charlyne Mattox, Lydia Karabinech, and Megan Phlug also helped crochet some of the projects. Eve Ng, the math wiz, checked all of the technical illustrations and instructions, and Melanie Falick, my editor, generously offered the example of her own book *Kids Knitting* as inspiration, and guided me wisely. **Thank you all.**

Special thanks to all the kids who learned how to crochet and modeled the projects, to my first students at University Settlement Camp in Beacon, to Margrit Lohrer and Albrecht Pichler at Morehouse Farm for allowing me to shoot at their colorful yarn booth, to all the marvelous yarn companies whose generosity enabled me to design and create such colorful projects, and to Jonathan McElroy for his love and constant inspiration.

Index

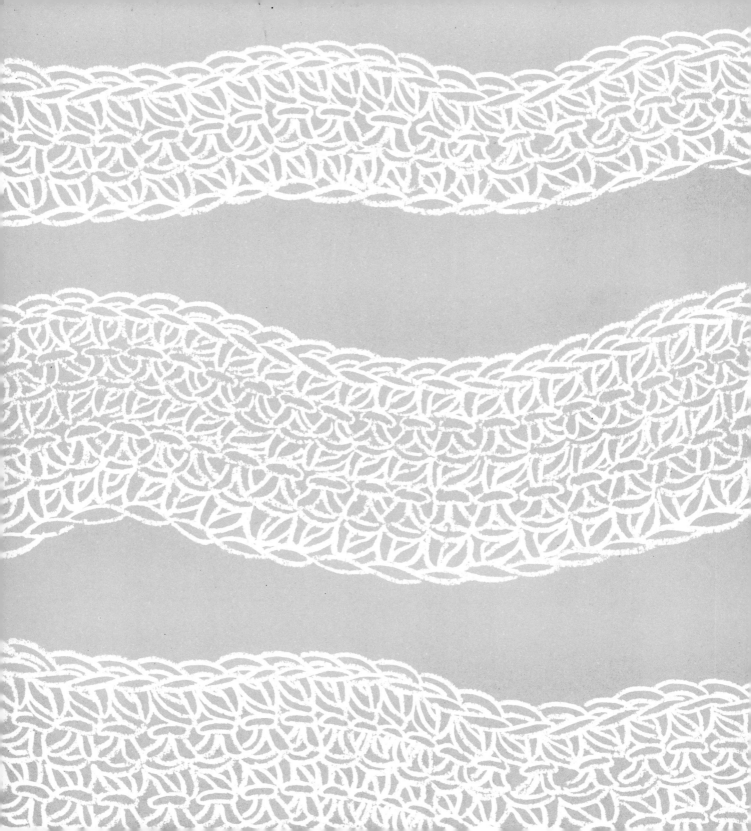